Series Authors
Karen Hume
Brad Ledgerwood

Series Consultants
Jennette MacKenzie, *Senior Consultant*
Damian Cooper, *Assessment*
James Coulter, *Assessment and Instruction*
Gayle Gregory, *Differentiated Instruction*
Ruth McQuirter Scott, *Word Study*

Series Writing Team
James Coulter, *Assessment*
Kathy Lazarovits, *ELL/ESL*
Liz Powell, *Instruction*
Sue Quennell, *Word Study*
Janet Lee Stinson, *Instruction*
Michael Stubitsch, *Instruction*

Subject and Specialist Reviewers
Mary Baratto, *The Arts*
Rachel Cooke, *Metacognition*
Phil Davison, *Media Literacy*
Graham Draper, *Geography*
Ian Esquivel, *Media Literacy*
Martin Gabber, *Science and Technology*
Cathy Hall, *Mathematics*
Jan Haskings-Winner, *History*
Dan Koenig, *Health*
Kathy Lazarovits, *ELL/ESL*
Janet Lee Stinson, *Media Literacy*

NELSON EDUCATION

NELSON EDUCATION

Nelson Literacy 7c

Director of Publishing
Kevin Martindale

General Manager, Literacy and Reference
Michelle Kelly

Director of Publishing, Literacy
Joe Banel

Executive Managing Editor, Development
Darleen Rotozinski

Senior Product Manager
Mark Cressman

Senior Program Manager
Diane Robitaille

Developmental Editors
Gillian Scobie
Marilyn Wilson

Researcher
Catherine Rondina

Assistant Editors
Corry Codner
Adam Rennie

Bias Reviewer
Nancy Christoffer

Editorial Assistants
Meghan Newton
Kristen Sanchioni

Executive Director, Content and Media Production
Renate McCloy

Director, Content and Media Production
Carol Martin

Senior Content Production Editor
Laurie Thomas

Content Production Editor
Natalie Russell

Proofreader
Elizabeth D'Anjou

Production Manager
Helen Jager Locsin

Production Coordinator
Vicki Black

Director, Asset Management Services
Vicki Gould

Design Director
Ken Phipps

Managing Designer
Sasha Moroz

Series Design
Sasha Moroz

Series Wordmark
Sasha Moroz

Cover Design
Sasha Moroz
Glenn Toddun

Interior Design
Carianne Bauldry
Jarrel Breckon
Nicole Dimson
Courtney Hellam
Jennifer Laing
Eugene Lo
Sasha Moroz
Peter Papayanakis
Jan John Rivera
Carrie Scherkus
Industrial Strength

Art Buyer
Suzanne Peden

Compositor
Courtney Hellam

Photo Research and Permissions
Nicola Winstanley

Printer
Transcontinental Printing

Advisers and Reviewers

Gwen Babcock

Jennifer Bach

Karen Beamish

Mary Cairo

Joanna Cascioli

Vivian Collyer

Anne Converset

Rachel Cooke

Phil Davison

Lori Driussi

Judy Dunn

Eileen Eby

Ian Esquivel

Patty Friedrich

Anna Filice-Gagliardi

Charmaine Graves

Colleen Hayward

Brenda Lightburn

Andrew Locker

Susan MacDonald

Anne Marie McDonald

Selina Millar

Wanda Mills-Boone

Lorellie Munson

Barb Muron

Linda O'Reilly

Cathy Pollock

Gina Rae

Susan Stevens

Janet Lee Stinson

Melisa Strimas

Laurie Townshend

Tracy Toyama

Deborah Tranton-Waghorn

Ann Varty

Ruth Wiebe

Nadia Young

CONTENTS

Unit 5 — Send a Message

8

16

21

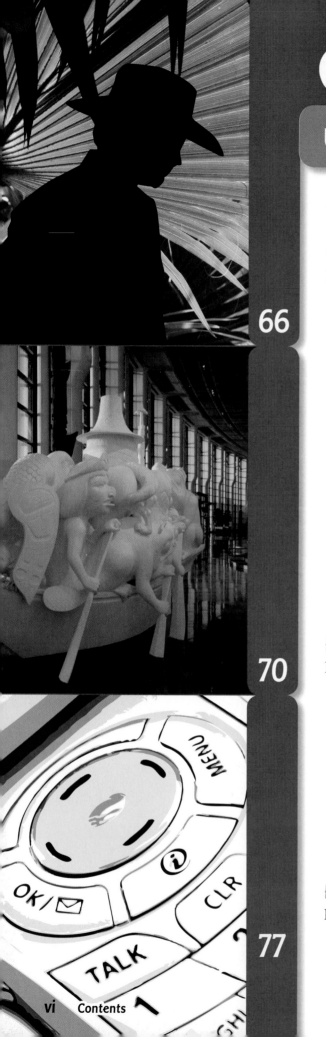

66

70

77

CONTENTS

Unit 6 — Make an Impression

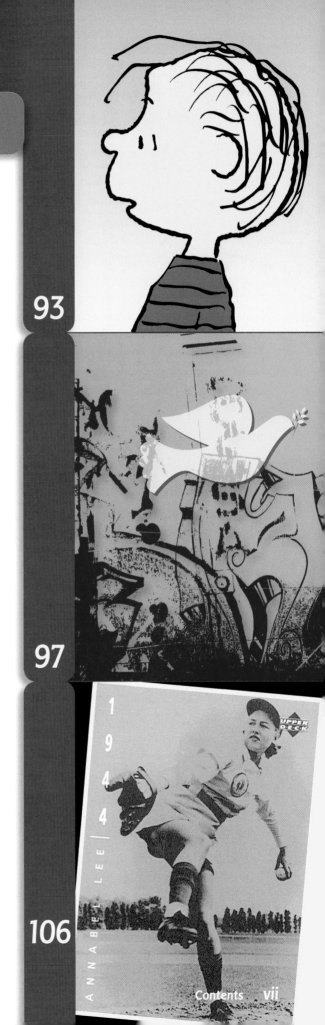

Welcome to
Nelson Literacy

Nelson Literacy presents a rich variety of literature, informational articles, and media texts from Canada and around the world. Many of the selections offer tips to help you develop strategies in reading, oral communication, writing, and media literacy.

Here are the different kinds of pages you will see in this book:

Focus pages

These pages outline a specific strategy and describe how to use it. Included are "Transfer Your Learning" tips that show how you can apply that strategy to other strands and subjects.

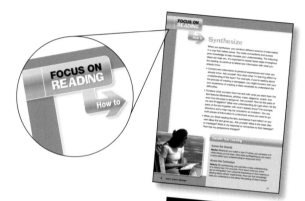

Understanding Strategies

These selections have instructions in the margins that help you to understand and use reading, writing, listening, speaking, and media literacy strategies.

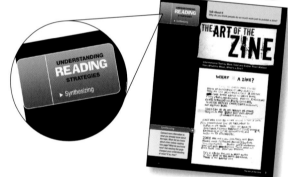

Applying Strategies

These selections give you the chance to apply the strategies you have learned. You will see a variety of formats and topics.

Transfer Your Learning

At the end of the unit, you'll have a chance to see how the strategies you have learned can help you in other subject areas such as Science and Technology, Geography, History, Health, Mathematics, and the Arts.

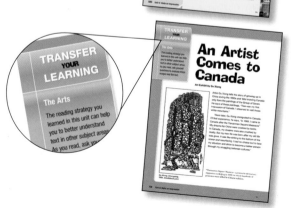

SEND A MESSAGE

What do you think are the most effective ways to send a message?

Unit Learning Goals

- synthesize while reading
- improve fluency in writing
- synthesize while listening
- analyze elements of media texts
- identify cause-and-effect text patterns

Transfer Your Learning: History

How to ▶ Synthesize

When you synthesize, you combine different sources of information in a way that makes sense. You make connections and access prior knowledge to help increase your understanding. The following steps can help you. It's important to repeat these steps throughout the reading, to continue to blend new information with what you already know.

• Connect new information to personal experiences and what you already know. Ask yourself: How does what I'm learning affect my understanding of the topic? For example, if you're reading about the process of creating a newspaper, you might connect with your own experience of creating a class newsletter to understand the difficulties.

• Combine what you learn from the text with what you learn from the text features (illustrations, photos, maps, diagrams, charts, and even how the page is designed). Ask yourself: How do the parts of the text fit together? What new understanding do I get when I fit the parts of the text together with what I already know? For example, directions and a map may be included in an invitation. You use both pieces of information to understand where you need to go.

• When you finish reading the text, summarize it and reflect on any new ideas the text gives you. Ask yourself: What is the main idea or message? What is my response or connection to that message? How has my perspective changed?

Transfer Your Learning

Across the Strands

Media: Whenever you watch a new TV show, you compare it to other shows you've seen. How does synthesizing as you watch a show affect your understanding or enjoyment of it?

Across the Curriculum

History: By synthesizing, you can form a new understanding of a history text. For example, think about what you know about immigration from personal experience or from hearing or reading about others' experiences. How can that knowledge help you understand a text about the settling of New France?

Talk About It
Why do you think people do so much work just to publish a zine?

THE ART OF THE ZINE

Informational Text by Mark Todd and Esther Pearl Watson
from *Whatcha Mean, What's a Zine?*

Synthesizing

→

Connect new information to what you already know about the topic. What did you know about zines before reading this page? What do you know now? Has reading this page changed your understanding of zines? If so, how?

WHAT'S A ZINE?

ZINES ARE CHEAPLY MADE PRINTED FORMS OF EXPRESSION ON ANY SUBJECT. THEY ARE LIKE MINI-MAGAZINES OR HOMEMADE COMIC BOOKS ABOUT FAVOURITE BANDS, Funny STORIES, SUB-CULTURES, PERSONAL COLLECTIONS COMIX ANTHOLOGIES, DIARY ENTRIES, PATHETIC REPORT CARDS, CHAIN RESTAURANTS, AND ANYTHING ELSE.

ZINES CAN BE BY ONE PERSON OR MANY. THEY CAN BE ANY SIZE: HALF PAGE, ROLLED UP, QUARTER SIZED. . . .

ZINES ARE READ BY ANYONE WILLING TO TAKE A LOOK, FROM CONCERT-GOERS AND THE MAIL MAN TO PEOPLE ON THE TRAIN. THEY ARE SOLD AT BOOKSTORES, TRUMBED THROUGH AT ZINE LIBRARIES, EXCHANGED AT COMIC CONVENTIONS, AND MAILED OFF TO STRANGERS.

ZINES ARE NOT A NEW IDEA. THEY HAVE BEEN AROUND UNDER DIFFERENT NAMES (CHAPBOOKS, PAMPHLETS, FLYERS). PEOPLE WITH INDEPENDENT IDEAS HAVE BEEN GETTING THEIR WORD OUT SINCE THERE WERE PRINTING PRESSES.

IT'S A GREAT FEELING TO HOLD COPIES OF YOUR ZINE IN YOUR HAND. GO AHEAD, THERE IS NO WRONG WAY.

hesizing

ct new information to
nal experiences. What
ctions can you make
en your own experiences
e experiences of these
people?

Ron Regé, Jr

I started making weird little minicomics mostly because I was working at a copy shop and could make them for free. I had a post office box and started to get five to ten pieces of artsy little books a week. I could take a day or two out of every month to fill orders, and create lovely packages to send to all the great people around the world.

Saelee Oh

My first zine was some embarrassing thing that I made in high school and I only made about ten copies but gave away even less that that. It probably made sense to nobody but me. I am a sucker for books with handmade touches like collage, original drawings, stitching, and so on.

Jeffrey Brown

The great thing about zines is they're expected to lose money, so you get a purity to the art that rarely happens elsewhere in "normal" publishing. Of course, sometimes you get what you pay for.

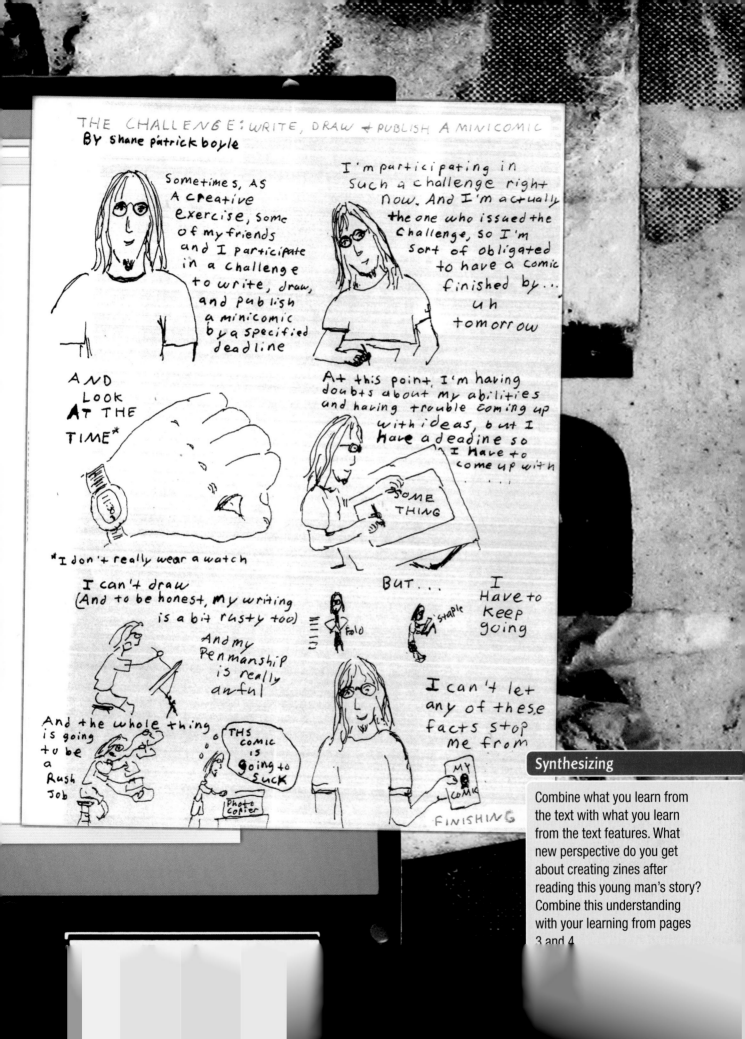

Synthesizing

Combine what you learn from the text with what you learn from the text features. What new perspective do you get about creating zines after reading this young man's story? Combine this understanding with your learning from pages 3 and 4

So, what's it gonna be? Pull up a chair, put your feet on the table, and let your mind wander. Topics could be about anything, as important as the meaning of life, or as dull as the insoles of your shoes.

Making lists is a good start. List the places you have lived, the people you have met at the copy store, meals you have shared with others, neighbours, or bad movies to laugh at.

You don't have to be an artist. Use collage elements to dress up the look of your zine. You don't have to draw the art yourself, you can work with someone who loves to draw. It doesn't matter if you are all words or all art, you just have to have a voice, an attitude, and something to say!

Access to a copy machine and a long-arm stapler wouldn't hurt either.

CAN'T START?

Afraid you won't finish? Then zine about never being able to finish. Think no one would be interested in what you have to say? Zine for yourself! Letting go of your fears may help you break free of creative blocks. Break larger goals down into little ones. It builds confidence to accomplish smaller projects like a four-page zine instead of a 64-page one. It also helps to tune out the critic inside your head while you're working.

Every time you make a new zine, you get better and faster, and learn tricks.

Synthesizing

Continue to blend new information with what you already know and what you're learning. What does this information add to your understanding of zines?

How do you become inspired?

★ Collect zines you like.

★ Look at places that no one else looks at for ideas.

★ Look at what is around you for ideas.

★ Challenge yourself.

★ Keep your eyes and ears open. Look up; look down; look around.

★ Sometimes it's the process of zine making that is the art, not the finished product. Enjoy the struggle and accidents that occur.

★ Don't be afraid to take on a task that's too big. You can make disposable zines as warm-ups.

★ Do something out of character. Do something that makes you say, "I'm going to regret this!"

← **Synthesizing**

After you've finished reading, summarize the text and reflect on any new ideas the text gives you. How has reading this text changed your understanding of zines?

Synthesizing

Use a graphic organizer like this one to help you as you synthesize.

Events or Information in the Text	What I Already Know	What I Think Now

Reflecting

Synthesizing: After reading this text, how have your ideas on zines changed? What caused the change?

Metacognition: If you had the choice of communicating your understanding of a topic through any form of media, would you choose a zine? Think about your own strengths and weaknesses. Would you be a good zine publisher?

Critical Literacy: What audience is this selection written for: teens or adults? How has the intended audience affected the text?

Talk About It

What medium are you most likely to use to get the news? Newspapers? Radio? TV? The Internet?

THE POWER OF THE PRESS

Article by Clive Gifford

Many adults read some form of newspaper regularly, and newspapers can have a great influence on public opinion. Powerful newspaper owners frequently try to affect the way that events are reported. Most newspapers have particular viewpoints, and journalists may choose to slant stories to reflect these outlooks. Some may even go as far as altering photos to make events suit their own purposes. And almost all newspapers treat the achievements of their own country as especially important.

The News in 1912

Before the arrival of radio, newsreels, and TV, major events, such as the tragic tale of the sinking of the *Titanic* in 1912, **left**, were brought to the world by newspapers alone.

Paper Popularity

The circulation of newspapers has declined since the 1950s as more and more people get their news from radio, TV, and the Internet. Some newspapers have attempted to win readers by becoming more like magazines.

In Canada we have a couple of national newspapers and thousands of local community newspapers. Some newspapers come out every day and others come out once a week. Some are quite large, with several different sections, and others are quite small with no more than 30 pages.

Front Page, Soviet-Style

On April 12, 1961, the Soviet cosmonaut Yuri Gagarin became the first person in space. The U.S.A. and USSR had been involved in a "space race" since 1957, and this event was a great triumph for the Soviet Union. The story took up the national newspaper *Izvestiya's* entire front page. The paper covered all aspects of the event, including a description of the flight, a report from the landing place, and a history of the Soviet Union's space program.

Headline interprets the space flight as a great victory for socialism.

Letter of congratulation to Gagarin from Soviet leader Khruschev

Picture of Yuri Gagarin dominates front page.

Report from the landing place

Front Page, American-Style

The front page of *The New York Times* on April 12, 1961, was very different from *Izvestiya*. Although the Soviet Union's space flight is the main story, it jostles for space on the page with many others, and there is no photo of Yuri Gagarin. The reporter has kept to the bare facts of the story, which are related in a low-key tone. The first person in space was an event of worldwide significance—but it was a political triumph only for the Soviet Union.

Photo of the trial of a former Nazi has been chosen over one of Gagarin.

Just one column out of eight is devoted to the space flight.

Supporting story focuses on U.S. space tracking stations.

Making News

Some events, such as wars, natural disasters, and serious crimes, become major news stories and are always reported widely by newspapers, radio, TV, and the Internet. But there is often a demand for unusual, small-scale tales that appeal to human emotions. Sometimes, a local story is picked up by national newspapers and TV and even becomes international news. When this happens, a modest event can snowball to involve a large media network, from local reporters to international news corporations. This was the case with the tale of two pigs that saved their bacon when they escaped from their owner in Malmesbury, Wiltshire, England, in 1998.

1. The Owner's Tale

In January 1998, two Ginger Tamworth boars escaped from their owner, farmer Arnoldo Dijulio, on their way to the slaughterhouse. By the time they were recaptured, the pigs had become so famous that Mr. Dijulio was able to sell them for $24 000 to a national newspaper. Had he sold them at the slaughterhouse, they would have fetched $128.

2. The Local News

Local reporters are often on the lookout for strange or funny events in their own areas. When the Tamworth pigs escaped, local journalists wasted no time in investigating the event. Usually, when a newsworthy event takes place, a reporter, often accompanied by a photographer, is sent out to obtain details and quotes from eyewitnesses in order to put the full story together.

The Grunt Escape

map detailing the pigs' escape route

3. National Press

The story of the two pigs, now nicknamed the Tamworth Two, appeared in the national press. Newspapers, such as *The Daily Mail*, set out to capture public attention by writing and headlining the story in an entertaining way, and by going over details of the event as if it were serious news. The British public loved the story of the two escaped pigs. Animal sanctuaries volunteered to give the pair a home for life, and offers of cash came in from all over England.

4. Public Interest

When a story arouses public interest, news media respond by running more features and follow-up stories linked to the subject. Sometimes, media attention can itself become the news. News teams from Europe and the United States came to report on the British media's surprising interest in the story, rather than the actual tale of the two fugitive pigs.

In the dead of night, a member of the public tries to grab one of the pigs.

5. International Press

Lighthearted stories, such as this one, prove especially popular when much of the international news is gloomy. Before long, the story of the runaway pigs and the media interest in them had made the news in much of Europe, Japan, and New Zealand.

6. International TV Coverage

The US broadcasting channel NBC sent a film crew to Malmesbury to report on the Tamworth Two. Their story was sent back via satellite to the NBC newsroom in the United States, and it was featured as a news bulletin.

7. One Year Later

In 1999, the two pigs enjoyed an anniversary party held in their honour. They are living proof of how news-making can create celebrities—even out of pigs! The two have been called upon to appear in public, and furry-toy Tamworth Two pigs have been produced.

Reflecting

Synthesizing: What new understanding of the role of the press have you gained from reading this selection?

Metacognition: Why do you think it is important after reading a text to reflect on how your thinking has changed or how new information fits with what you already know?

Media Literacy: What criteria do you think editors use to determine which stories will appear on the front page of a newspaper? What criteria would you use?

APPLYING
READING
STRATEGIES

▸ Synthesizing

Talk About It

How do you respond when a relative gives you a gift that you don't really want?

The Thank-You Letter[1]

Letter by John Grandits

Dear Aunt Hildegard,

Thank you[2] for the amazing gifts.[3] It was terrific[4] getting your package![5] I grabbed it immediately.[6] But when my parents saw it,[7] they said[8] I shouldn't open it until my birthday. You can imagine how I felt when I found two gifts![9] The sweater was totally awesome.[10] It's amazing how well you know me.[11]

Then there was the poster you got for my room.[12] You're in luck; I don't already have a Polka Hall of Fame poster.[13] I'm putting it right under my World Wrestling Federation poster.[14]

Thanks,[15] thanks,[16] and thanks again.[17] I'm already planning when to wear my new sweater.[18]

Your 11-year-old[19] nephew,

Robert

1. With Footnotes

2. For nothing!

3. Do you have the slightest clue what an 11-year-old boy likes?

4. I almost croaked when I saw the package. I still remember last year's gift. "Oh, no! Not again!" I screamed.

5. I was in luck. Mom didn't see the mail carrier.

6. I hid the package in the garage under the hose.

7. What were the chances that Dad would decide to wash the car that day?

8. "What's this?" they said. "When did this come?"

9. You monster.

10. In the history of sweaters, there has never been an uglier waste of yarn.

11. Where did you ever find a sweater that not only has Barney on it, but also is two sizes too big for me?

12. I'm old enough to decorate my own room.

13. Just what I need—a picture of an old guy with an accordion.

14. And I do mean UNDER.

15. For trying to embarrass me in front of my friends.

16. For the lectures from my parents.

17. For making me waste an hour of my life writing this stupid thank-you letter.

18. I know they'll make me wear it the next time you come to visit. I just hope nobody sees me.

19. I'm 11!!! Get it?!?

Reflecting

Synthesizing: What's your impression of the person writing the letter? What information did you use to form this impression? What prior experience helped you form that impression?

Metacognition: To understand the letter fully, you had to read the letter with each note. In fact, it probably helped if you read the letter and notes more than once. How did synthesizing as you read this selection help you understand it?

Critical Literacy: Some people feel that the thank-you letter is no longer necessary. Others feel that the thank-you letter is a lost art. What is the letter-writer's view on thank-you letters? How can you tell?

Talk About It
What are some of the pros and cons of creating a blog?

The Blogger From Iraq

Online Interview by Lakshmi Chaudhry

On August 17, 2003, Riverbend posted the first entry of her blog, where she introduced herself to her readers: "I'm female, Iraqi, and 24. I survived the war. That's all you need to know. It's all that matters these days anyway."

She responded to these interview questions via e-mail from her home in Baghdad.

Lakshmi: Let's start with the obvious. Why did you start writing a blog?

Riverbend: After the war, an acquaintance, Salam Pax, suggested I should start my own blog as I could write in English and after thinking about it for a while, I eventually did. I liked the idea of blogging because I was very frustrated with the Western media for telling only half of the story in Iraq. No one seemed to know what was going on inside of the country—all the damage and horror Iraqis were facing on a daily basis.

In addition to this, blogging proved to be therapeutic. It was a way to vent fears and anger that I couldn't really express in front of family and friends because it was always necessary to stay strong and, to some extent, positive.

Lakshmi: Reading your blog entries, it's obvious that some of your audience is not Iraqi. Was this your original intention or did it just turn out that way?

Riverbend: I don't think I wrote the blog for any particular audience. I simply wanted to express my emotions and thoughts and I wasn't sure who would read it. I never expected many Iraqis inside of Iraq to read it because Iraqis are far too busy coping with daily realities to read blogs or even write them. I liked blogging in English because it's a language people in many different countries understand.

Lakshmi: What role does the blog play in your life today, especially given its immense success?

Riverbend: The blog for a while became a part of my daily life. I began seeing things from a blogging point of view in many situations and wondering what the readers would think if they could do or see what I was currently doing or seeing! My family is sometimes curious about it, but more often than not, they worry about my safety. I try to make time for reading and answering e-mails and sometimes blogging, but it all depends on the electricity/phone situation.

Lakshmi: Finally, what are your hopes for the future—both for your nation and in your own life?

Riverbend: My hopes for the future are like those of millions of Iraqis. I hope for a peaceful, independent, secure country. I also hope for prosperity for the millions of Iraqis who certainly deserve it after all of these hardships. I think if Iraq can have the above, there'll be nothing lacking in my life personally.

Read these two sample blogs from Riverbend.

SEARCH NEXT

Friday, December 29, 2006

End of Another Year

… A day in the life of the average Iraqi has been reduced to identifying corpses, avoiding car bombs, and attempting to keep track of which family members have been detained, which ones have been exiled, and which ones have been abducted….

This last year especially has been a turning point. Nearly every Iraqi has lost so much. So much. There's no way to describe the loss we've experienced with this war and occupation. There are no words to relay the feelings that come with the knowledge that daily almost 40 corpses are found. There is no compensation for the dense, black cloud of fear that hangs over the head of every Iraqi. Fear of things so out of one's hands, it borders on the ridiculous—like whether your name is "too Sunni" or "too Shia." Fear of the larger things—like the Americans in the tank, the police patrolling your area in black bandanas and green banners, and the Iraqi soldiers wearing black masks at the checkpoint….

Saturday, August 05, 2006

Summer of Goodbyes

… I've said goodbye this last month to more people than I can count. Some of the "goodbyes" were hurried and furtive—the sort you say at night to the neighbour who got a death threat and is leaving at the break of dawn, quietly.

Some of the "goodbyes" were emotional and long-drawn, to the relatives and friends who can no longer bear to live in a country coming apart at the seams.

Many of the "goodbyes" were said stoically—almost casually—with a fake smile plastered on the face and the words, "See you soon"… only to walk out the door and want to collapse with the burden of parting with yet another loved one.

I sometimes wonder if we'll ever know just how many hundreds of thousands of Iraqis left the country this bleak summer. I wonder how many of them will actually return. Where will they go? What will they do with themselves? Is it time to follow? Is it time to wash our hands of the country and try to find a stable life somewhere else?

Reflecting

Synthesizing: How does this selection help you look differently at the situation in Iraq?

Metacognition: In this selection you read an interview and a few blog entries, and you also viewed photos. How does using different types and kinds of information help you synthesize information and gain a new perspective?

Critical Literacy: There are pros and cons to using first-hand accounts when you research. What other documents would you need to support your research if you were researching the conflict in Iraq?

How to → Improve Fluency

Language has rhythm and flow. When we enjoy someone's writing, it is often because we hear the words in our mind as clearly as if someone were speaking to us. Writing that flows is described as *fluent*.

A fluent writer

- uses sentences that are varied in length

- uses sentences that are varied in structure (for example, a good writer varies the positions of nouns and verbs; uses simple, compound, and complex sentences and uses statements, questions, and exclamations)

- varies the beginnings of sentences

- makes limited but effective use of transition words or phrases, such as *for example*, *however*, and *therefore*

- uses dialogue that sounds authentic (usually just in fiction)

Check your writing for fluency by reading it aloud. Revise and reread it until your writing sounds right to you.

Check out how Samantha has edited her story to make it more fluent.

Jake wanted ∧nothing but video games for his birthday. ~~Jake wanted video games for his bar mitzvah.~~ ~~Jake wanted video games for~~ ∧and his graduation. ∧Unfortunately, Jake didn't tell anyone ∧what he wanted ∧video games. ∧So, can you guess what happened? Jake got socks from his parents. ~~Jake got socks from his grandparents.~~ ~~Jake got socks from~~ and even ∧his best friend. Jake got nothing but socks! "Thank you very much," said Jake.
∧'s a lot!

Transfer Your Learning

Across the Strands

Oral Language: What strategies do you use to make sure your oral presentations are not choppy?

Across the Curriculum

History: When you write a history paper, how do you make sure your writing is fluent?

Talk About It
What are some characteristics of a good spy?

Communication,

Spy-Style

**Instructional Text from *Secret Agent Y.O.U.*
by Helaine Becker**

➡ You did it! You've got the top-secret plans of the enemy's space pod facility. All that remains now is for you to get them to your contact, Penelope Pluto.

Easier said than done. The enemy is everywhere, watching your every move. How will you get the plans to Pluto? In this confidential communiqué, you will be briefed on everything you need to master the art and science of communication, spy-style.

Identifying Your Contact

As an agent in the field, Y.O.U. have never seen another member of your network. How will you recognize Agent Pluto when you meet?

Spies have developed many ingenious techniques for solving this identity dilemma. A secret password, known only by your allies, is one of the oldest tricks in the book.

Create Your Own Secret Password

Making a secret password for your own spy network is easy. Choose a word or phrase that is easy to remember. Don't write it down! You might consider selecting a word at random from the dictionary. Change your password frequently in case someone accidentally overhears you when you use it. For example, you might say, "The pheasant has taken the pudding." Your contact may respond, "The pudding is an elephant."

Let's Shake on It

A secret handshake is another great way to make sure your contact is who he or she is supposed to be. The best kind is one that both hand-shakers can feel, but others can't see. It should also be subtle, so if it turns out you have the wrong person, nobody will catch on to what you are doing.

Try this one, or modify it to make up your own. When you shake hands, tap the inside of the other person's palm with your pinky finger. His/her response should be to quickly squeeze your thumb.

If the other person does not respond correctly, return your finger to its normal position and continue with a regular handshake.

Fluency

Fluent writers use authentic dialogue, usually just in fiction. In this particular nonfiction text, why does it make sense that the dialogue sounds unnatural or odd?

The Mix 'n' Match Greeting

To guarantee that the right people connect, spies are sometimes given one half of an object, such as a ripped coupon or playing card. If the two halves match up, chances are good the meeting is safe.

The No-Meet Meet

Passwords and handshakes work well when you and your colleagues are all together. But how do you get your network together in the first place? You need a prearranged signal, one that does not rely on any of you being in the same place at the same time for sending and receiving it.

Get together with your spy network and agree ahead of time on your meeting place (say, your backyard). Next, choose a method for contacting each other and what each signal will mean. Try these methods:

Make a chalk mark on the sidewalk outside of your meeting place. A green chalk mark means "Meet in my backyard after school." A red chalk mark might mean "My backyard is closed today."

Leave a newspaper or comic book in the school library, opened to page 10, to tell your colleagues to get together at lunch.

A phony e-mail message with a signal embedded in it can be both effective and funny. Example: Address your e-mail to "My Dear Prairie Dogs" to let your spy network know you want to meet to welcome a new member.

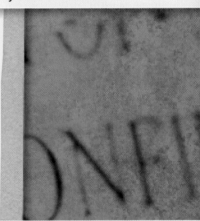

← Fluency

Fluent writers use sentences that are varied in structure. Note how this writer uses statements, questions, and commands. How would this paragraph sound if she had only used commands?

← Fluency

Fluent writers use sentences that are varied in structure. Note how this writer is using simple, complex, and compound sentences. How would this paragraph sound if she had only used simple sentences?

Delivering the Message

You've arranged the meet. Now you have to deliver the goods. The brush pass and the dead drop are two methods for trading secrets with your contact. Two methods with endless possibilities….

The Brush Pass

The brush pass is a lot like passing the baton in a relay race. It relies on good timing, excellent acting skills, solid planning, and a little bit of luck. Here are three agent-approved methods to try:

The Classic Klutz

Saunter past your contact on the street. Drop something, such as your notebook. Of course it has the message tucked inside the front cover. Your contact picks up the book and hands it back to you, while at the same time he/she removes the message.

The Fido

Fold your message so it fits under your dog's collar. Walk the dog. Meet your contact, who asks if she can pet the dog. You say yes, and when she does, she removes the message from the collar. Then you both continue in opposite directions.

Dead Drop

A dead drop is a prearranged location where you leave the secret goodies for your contact to retrieve later. Almost any place can be used for a dead drop. For a dead drop to work, choose your location carefully. It should not be likely to be disturbed by other people or animals. If it is outside, it must be protected from the elements.

Hiding Messages

Savvy field agents need to know how to conceal their secret messages.

The Double Decker

With this double-crosser of a card trick, you can deliver secret documents (a letter or a map) right under the Queen of Hearts' nose!

You'll Need

- secret document
- pencil
- ruler
- scissors
- glue stick

- two identical decks of standard playing cards (make sure no one will ever want to use them again—they will get ruined)

Spy Science: Figuring out how to hide messages is not only an art, but it's an actual science! Its scientific name is *steganography*. The term comes from the Greek words *stegano* (hidden) and *graph* (writing).

1. Cut your secret document into rectangles 6 cm x 8 cm. Each piece should be slightly smaller than a playing card.

2. Collect a matching pair of cards from the two decks for each piece of your document. Set the remaining cards of one deck aside. Carefully glue one piece of the document onto the face of a card from each pair. Allow to dry ten minutes.

3. Apply a thin layer of glue to the exposed edges of the card. (You want the glue to hold, but it should still be easy enough for your contact to separate the cards.) Carefully lay the matching card face side up over the document to make a sandwich.

4. Let the glue dry completely (about twenty minutes). Then insert the secret cards back into the deck you set aside in step 2.

5. Deliver the deck to your contact.

Your contact can then go through the deck and find the thicker cards, separate the two halves of the sandwich, and reassemble the message!

← **Fluency**

Fluent writers vary the beginnings of sentences. Many of the sentences in this section are commands. Imagine how boring this section would sound if, instead of different verbs, each command began with the words *you have to*.

Newspaper Pin-Prick Message

What's more common than a daily newspaper? No one will suspect a thing if you pass on a message using a free community newspaper.

You'll Need

- paper & pencil
- newspaper
- safety pin

1. Write out a draft of your message on the piece of paper.

2. Find a day-old newspaper. Look for an example of each word in your message—this will be easier for you and your contact if the message is brief and simple.

3. Using the safety pin, prick a tiny hole underneath each of the words. Try to keep the words in the same order as the words in your message.

4. Give the newspaper to your contact (consider a brush pass or dead drop). All he/she has to do is hold the paper up to the light to find the pinholes and read your message.

Fact File

The Navajo Code Talkers

The Navajo language is so complex that no one but a native Navajo speaker can really get it right. During World War II, the Navajo language was used as a communication code. The Allied forces recruited Navajo speakers to work as radio operators. Their back-and-forth messages—many of them containing critical information about troop movements—were plainly heard by the enemy code breakers. It didn't matter. The enemy couldn't even begin to decipher what was being said. The Navajo "code" was never broken.

Winged Warriors

During World Wars I and II, one of the most reliable ways to deliver messages was by using homing pigeons. These winged soldiers were specially outfitted with unbreakable, lightweight canisters for the notes. Messages had to be very short (tissue-thin paper was used for maps), and codes were often written in teensy type. Some birds even received medals for valour. Amazingly, nearly all of the pigeons sent through enemy fire completed their missions.

Message Will Self-Destruct in 10 ... 9 ... 8 ...

A service available to cellphone subscribers allows them to send messages that, like time bombs, blow up! The service is for people who want to send sensitive information, but are afraid that it might fall into the wrong hands. Intelligence sent using "stealthtext" erases itself after 40 s, leaving no trace for snoops.

Please Enter Your Password

Passwords are useful outside of your secret agent work too. For example, passwords are vital when you work online to protect your e-mail accounts, your Internet transactions, even your very identity.

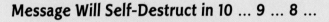

When choosing a password for the Internet, don't use something easy to guess like your nickname, the name of your pet, or your birthday. Pick a word or number at random, but one that you can remember easily. Don't share it with anyone (except your parents, of course)!

← **Fluency**

Fluent writers use transition words. How does the use of transitions affect the fluency of this paragraph?

Reflecting

Reading Like a Writer: Think of the different aspects of fluent reading listed on page 20. If you were a peer editor for Helaine Becker, the author of the selection, which aspect would you tell her she had used effectively? Where would you suggest some changes?

Metacognition: How does thinking about someone else's fluent writing help you improve your writing?

Talk About It

In a life-and-death situation, what is the best way to communicate with rescuers?

Emergency Communication

Article by Clive Gifford

A warning message may help to prevent an accident. And if a disaster arises, quick and accurate communication can help save lives.
The stricken victims need to let others know of their predicament so that assistance can be organized. Rescuers need to communicate with each other and with the victims, often in hazardous conditions.
Before the arrival of advanced communication devices, such as light-weight radios and mobile phones, many ingenious methods, from flares to flags, were used to warn people of approaching danger or to announce distress.

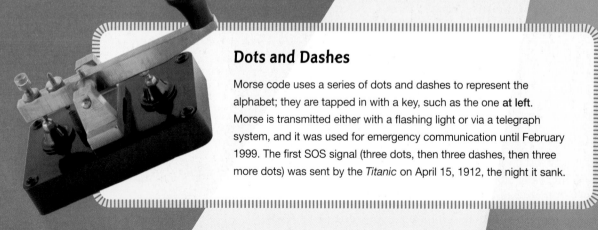

Dots and Dashes

Morse code uses a series of dots and dashes to represent the alphabet; they are tapped in with a key, such as the one **at left**. Morse is transmitted either with a flashing light or via a telegraph system, and it was used for emergency communication until February 1999. The first SOS signal (three dots, then three dashes, then three more dots) was sent by the *Titanic* on April 15, 1912, the night it sank.

The light from this lighthouse is visible from 25 km.

Warning Lights

Lighthouses and lightships have been used for centuries to warn sailors of rocks or shallow seas. They are still used as warnings for marine craft, but today most are uncrewed.

Telephone Gas Mask

Communication channels must be kept open whenever there is an emergency or disaster. During wartime, special equipment is often called for. This World War II headgear, for example, combined a gas mask with a telephone operator's headset, so that telephone calls, especially vital ones, could still be made, even in the event of a major release of harmful gas.

Telephone operator's gas mask, made in 1938

Message-receiving headphones

Operator's mouthpiece

Filter prevents inhalation of noxious fumes

This semaphore signaller is spelling out the word H-E-L-P.

Flags are always held with the arms extended so that they can be clearly seen

Flags are always held with the arms extended so that they can be clearly seen

Flag Signals

A system of communicating with flags, known as *semaphore*, was invented and developed in the 18th century by a French schoolboy, Claude Chappé. Two flags are held in different positions to represent the letters of the alphabet. Semaphore was later adopted for ship-to-shore and some land communications.

Flagging a Problem

Flags have been used for many centuries to communicate basic messages from hilltop to hilltop and between ships at sea. A standardized system for maritime flags was introduced in the 19th century. The flags represent both letters and numbers and have particular meanings. For example, the flag shown here means "You are steering toward the centre of a typhoon."

Flares and Foghorns

Flares and foghorns are used to communicate distress and indicate location for a search or rescue party. Foghorns use compressed air from a cylinder to make an ear-piercing noise. Flares are either handheld or launched into the air and burn brightly for several minutes

Handheld flares burn with an orange, red, or white light.

Warning Signs

Simple pictures or symbols are used all over the world to convey easily recognizable warnings. They have been devised to alert people to the dangers of harmful materials or equipment. These symbols, such as those pictured here, are often seen on freight carriers or in factories and laboratories.

radioactive

toxic/poisonous

Reflecting

Reading Like a Writer: In your opinion, is fluency more difficult to achieve when the text is written in small chunks or when it is written as a longer piece? What evidence from this selection supports your answer?

Synthesizing: Has your view about how well-prepared you are for a crisis changed as a result of reading this article? If so, what information changed your perspective?

Talk About It
Disaster strikes … what message do you send?

MESSAGES
IN THE
FACE OF DISASTER

Informational Report by Vicky Zhong

B.C. Ferry Sinks—Eyewitness Reports

It is March 23, 2006, and a ferry carries 101 passengers from Vancouver Island to British Columbia's northern coast. It's a rough, rainy night. The only warnings of trouble are a grating noise, a loud bang, and the lights going out. Passengers and crew scramble into lifeboats. Half an hour later, the *Queen of the North* sinks. Two people die in the disaster.

One survivor, Jill Lawrence, reports, "We were in bed. I thought we were docking or something like that. It didn't seem like it was too much of a bump to me. And then, the next thing you know, when I looked down, everything was all over the floor. We heard the alarm go. So we jumped out of bed and got out."

One rescuer, 16-year-old Karl Fisher, reports, "I just see the boat floating there and all the lights are on. All the life rafts are all tied up together, drifting away. Then it started sinking and it just kept going.… You could just hear all the cars in the carport crashing down on each other. When it went straight up and down you could hear every one just hit. It was loud."

The Halifax Explosion—A Life-Saving Message

December 6, 1917, two ships collide and explode in the Halifax Harbour. Over 1900 people die. Over 9000 people are injured. Instead of fleeing and saving himself, Vince Coleman, a train dispatcher, sends out a vital telegraph message to an incoming passenger train. He sacrifices his life to save 700 other people. His message? "Stop trains. Munitions ship on fire. Approaching Pier 6. Goodbye boys."

The explosion as seen from over 20 km away. This is probably the only photo of this tragic event.

The *Titanic* Sinks—CQD and SOS

April 15, 1912, the *Titanic* slowly sinks after hitting an iceberg. Over 1500 people die. Over 700 people are rescued. Jack Phillips, the radio operator on the *Titanic*, starts out using CQD (the first radio distress signal) but later switches to the new SOS signal. Harold Cottam, the wireless operator on the ship RMS *Carpathia*, hears the distress message, but his ship (one of the closest) is too far away to provide assistance quickly enough. In the message below, *OM* stands for "old man."

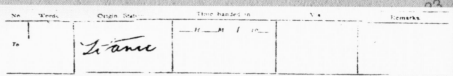

12:10 a.m. The first messages between the *Titanic* and *Carpathia*.
Titanic: Come at once. We have struck a berg. It's a CQD OM. Position 41.46 N. 50.14 W.
Carpathia: Shall I tell my Captain? Do you require assistance?
Titanic: Yes, come quick.

1:45 a.m. Last message from *Titanic* to *Carpathia*
Titanic: Come as quickly as possible old man: the engine-room is filling up to the boilers.

CQD means "all stations attend: distress," (it does not, as some people assume, stand for "come quickly, danger"). On the other hand, SOS stands for nothing; the letters were chosen because they were easy to tap out using Morse code.

At 2:20 a.m. the ship sinks, 2 hours and 40 minutes after hitting the iceberg.

Hindenburg Disaster—The Radio Report

On May 6, 1937, in Lakehurst, New Jersey, Herbert Morrison, a radio reporter, witnesses the explosion of the airship *Hindenburg*. As it approaches land, the *Hindenburg* suddenly bursts into flames and crashes to the ground before his eyes. Thirty-six people die. The following text is part of his report.

"... It's burst into flames!... It's falling, it's crashing! Watch it! Watch it! Get out of the way! Get out of the way!... It's fire—and it's crashing!... Oh, my! Get out of the way, please! It's burning and bursting into flames; and the—and it's falling on the mooring mast. And all the folks agree that this is terrible; this is the worst of the worst catastrophes in the world.... It's flames.... Crashing, oh! Four or five hundred feet into the sky and it—it's a terrific crash, ladies and gentlemen. It's smoke and it's flames now; and the frame is crashing to the ground, not quite to the mooring mast. Oh, the humanity. And all the passengers screaming around here.... Ah! It's— it—it's a—ah! I—I can't talk, ladies and gentlemen. Honest: it's just laying there, a mass of smoking wreckage. Ah! And everybody can hardly breathe and talk and the screaming. Lady, I—I—I'm sorry. Honest: I—I can hardly breathe. I—I'm going to step inside, where I cannot see it.... Ah, ah—I can't. Listen, folks; I—I'm gonna have to stop for a minute because I've lost my voice. This is the worst thing I've ever witnessed."

Reflecting

Reading Like a Writer: Look only at the paragraph that introduces each disaster, not the message. How effectively did this author use the different aspects of fluency listed on page 20?

Metacognition: What did you learn about writing fluently from reading this selection? What do you know about writing fluently that you would want to pass on to this writer?

Critical Literacy: This selection includes different types of texts: the paragraph that introduces each disaster, eyewitness accounts, telegraph messages, and a radio report, as well as photos. Why do you think different texts were included? How do you respond as a reader to those different texts?

How to Synthesize

Active listeners use specific strategies to synthesize an oral text and improve their understanding.

Follow these instructions to synthesize while you listen.	For example, if you were listening to a radio report about cyber bullying, this is how you might synthesize that text.
Make connections while you listen. Connections to personal knowledge and experience can help you make sense of what you are hearing.	When the reporter says, "One in four students is bullied," you might think of the students you know who have been bullied.
Compare what you are hearing with what you already know. Assess whether the information is important, true, or consistent with what you already know.	When she says, "Cyber bullying is on the rise in local schools," you might compare this information with what you know is happening at your school and realize, "Yes, that's true."
Contrast what you are hearing with what you already know. Assess information that is new, that challenges what you believe to be true. A focus on differences helps you learn new information and form new opinions.	When she says, "There seem to be no solutions!" You might contrast that information with what you know your school is doing, and think, "No, there *are* solutions."

Transfer Your Learning

Across the Strands

Reading: Compare the strategies listed here with the reading strategy of synthesizing. How is synthesizing while reading similar to synthesizing while listening? How is it different?

Across the Curriculum

History: History classes often have guest speakers, such as veterans. When you listen to a veteran, do you think you would make more comparisons or more contrasts to your personal experience?

Talk About It

What makes it easy—or hard—to communicate with your family?

Family Communication

Comic Strips from various sources

Synthesizing

Good listeners make connections. This comic strip creates humour by showing the bad connections that come from not listening carefully.

Adam@Home is a comic strip by Brian Basset.

Synthesizing

Good listeners compare and contrast what they're hearing with what they already know. Here, the son contrasts what the mother says about sugar in soft drinks with what he knows about soft drinks.

Zits is a comic strip by Jerry Scott and Jim Borgman.

Reflecting

Synthesizing: How do these comic strips demonstrate the importance of listening carefully and reconsidering what we know in the light of new information?

Metacognition: Think about a time that you had trouble understanding a speaker. What listening strategies would have helped you? How would you assess your ability to listen effectively?

Talk About It
What song lyrics have you been singing along to?

THERE'S A BATHROOM ON THE RIGHT

**Multimedia Presentation
by Karri Rivera**

In the following selection, Karri Rivera presents some information on the amusing interpretations of song lyrics.

Musical introduction, a medley of songs, including "Rock the Casbah," "Purple Haze," and "Bad Moon Rising."

KARRI: Do you love singing along to your favourite song? After you've heard a song over and over it seems like the words automatically pop out of your mouth. Are you *sure* the words you're hearing are what's *actually* being sung? Listen to this part of a song.

Play chorus of song "Rock the Casbah."

KARRI: Many people who listen to this song think the singer is saying, "Lock the cash box." He's actually singing "Rock the Casbah!" There are websites, TV shows, and even a board game devoted to misheard song lyrics. This chart shows some of the most popular.

PowerPoint presentation of chart, each line left and right flashing up, then disappearing. Karri sings each line the wrong and correct way.

Wrong	Correct
There's a bathroom on the right	There's a bad moon on the rise
Excuse me while I kiss this guy	Excuse me while I kiss the sky
Lock the cash box	Rock the Casbah
Tatoo detective	Try to detect it
My body lies over the ocean	My Bonnie lies over the ocean
Life's a butter dream	Life is but a dream

KARRI: These misheard song lyrics are called *mondegreens*. In fact two songwriters wrote a song full of mondegreens on purpose and called it "Mairzy Doats." The lyrics make no sense when you read them.

PowerPoint presentation to show two lines of song.

Mairzy doats and dozy doats and liddle lamzy divey

A kiddley divey too, wooden shoe?

KARRI: But when I play the song, you should hear words you understand.

Play recording of song.

KARRI: Words go from our ears to our brains and mix with experiences, expectations, familiar ideas, and familiar words. In the song "All Apologies," Kurt Cobain sang that he "found my nest of salt" but who's ever heard of a "nest of salt"?! It's no wonder people sang "found my nasty salt."

Play song "All Apologies."

Reflecting

Synthesizing: Think about how this student used a variety of tools—PowerPoint slides, song recordings, and her voice—to make her presentation. In listening to this presentation, what connections do you make? What new understanding do you reach?

Metacognition: As you listen and watch a PowerPoint presentation, which do you find it easier to follow: the spoken part or the part on screen? How can you use the strategy of synthesizing to help you understand both parts?

Connecting to Other Media: Do you ever read a song's lyrics online? Does watching a music video for a song help you understand its lyrics?

Talk About It
What does it take to change your mind about a person after you've formed a first impression?

THE WAY

Comic Strips by Lynn Johnston from *For Better Or For Worse*

I TALK

"Most cartoonists start the way I did: doodling on anything as soon as they were able to hold a pen. I've always loved to draw, and have always had a silly streak that more often than not, got me into trouble. *For Better Or For Worse* lets me put it to good use! I always knew I would be a cartoonist, but I never expected to make my LIVING as one!"

—Lynn Johnston

Reflecting

Synthesizing: What evidence is there that the audience in the comic strip synthesized while listening to the speaker?

Metacognition: We all have challenges that we try to overcome. What challenge have you overcome to make yourself a better student?

Critical Literacy: Why do you think Lynn Johnston created both of these comic strips? What effect do you think she wanted to have on her readers?

How to ▶ Analyze Media Elements

Media texts are designed to tell a certain story or to send a certain message. The power of the text is enhanced when different media elements are used and combined effectively. For example, in movies visual images are made even more powerful with the use of a good soundtrack, sound effects, or special effects.

The same approach of using various media elements can be found in textbooks. Traditional textbooks rely on limited media—mainly print—to send their message. However, many contemporary textbooks also use photos, cartoons, colourful layouts, and other media elements usually found in magazines.

For example, take a close look at this page from a *Nelson Literacy 7* magazine. Notice how it uses a variety of elements: photo, texture, paint splotch, title treatment, logo, boxed text, icon, and table of contents. These elements combine to create a powerful effect. Imagine how boring this page would look if the only elements were a plain title, plain text, and a photo of a shirt.

colourful tab

table of contents

icon

interesting logo

interesting title

paint splotch

boxed text

grunge texture

engaging photo

Some Questions to Ask as You Analyze Media Elements

- What is the **form of this media text**?

- What **media elements** does this text use?

- How effectively are these media elements used?

- What elements contribute to my enjoyment of this media text?

- What elements make this media text powerful (or not)?

- How are the elements of the media text combined to create or enhance meaning?

Media forms include things like newspapers, magazines, songs, movies, TV shows, maps, T-shirts, and so on.

The type of **media elements** in different forms can vary greatly. Movie elements, for example, include soundtracks, sound effects, special effects, flashbacks, dialogue, different types of shots, sets, costumes, and so on. Whereas, in magazines the usual media elements include photos, captions, illustrations, diagrams, maps, articles, questionnaires, headings, pull quotes, and so on.

Here's another example of a *Nelson Literacy 7* magazine. What media elements is it using? How effectively are those elements being used?

Transfer Your Learning

Across the Strands

Writing: Writers also combine different writing elements (for example, plot, character, humour, language) to enhance meaning. In the last book you read, what were some of the writing elements that helped you enjoy the book?

Across the Curriculum

Geography: Weather systems are interesting to watch on the Internet because you can see the weather developing. What are some of the media elements that are often found on weather websites? How do those elements combine to enhance the meaning of the text?

Talk About It
Why do you think manga cartoons are such an appealing media form?

WHAT'S MANGA?

Glossary by Chris Gwynne

What is manga anyway? How is it different from anime? Here's a quick guide to some of the words often used to describe manga.

anime *n*, [an-*uh*-mey]: Japanese word for animation. Many popular manga comics are adapted into animated movies, cartoons, or video games.

gekiga *n*, [geh-kie-gah]: serious manga comic books for an older audience. The style of art is more realistic. The word *gekiga* translates as "dramatic pictures."

manga *n*, [mahng-gah]: a Japanese comic book or graphic novel that uses fanciful images and covers a range of subjects and themes. The main style uses exaggerated, dramatic physical features such as large eyes, big hair, and lengthened limbs.

Analyzing Media Elements

Begin by identifying the media form. This selection includes examples of manga cartoons.

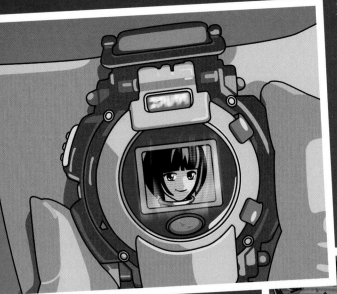

Analyzing Media Elements →

Identify the media elements the media text uses. Think about how these manga images use the elements listed in the definition for manga. How effectively are these elements used?

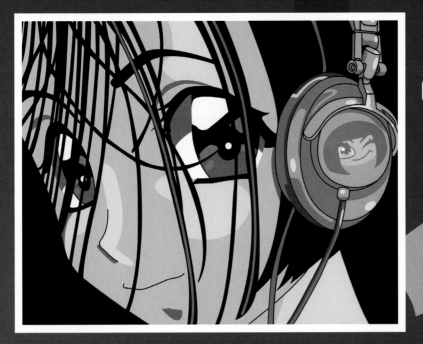

← Analyzing Media Elements

Identify the media elements that make the media text enjoyable or powerful. Refer to the media elements as you assess how enjoyable or powerful this example of manga art is.

mangaka *n*, [mahng-gah-kah]: someone who draws manga.

shoujo *n*, [show-joe]: a style of manga or anime intended for young women. Stories may be melodramatic or romantic and include a more flowery style of art.

shounen *n*, [show-nen]: a style of manga or anime intended for boys. Popular examples include *Dragon Ball* and *Fullmetal Alchemist*. This style includes a lot of action and humorous plots.

yonkoma *n*, [yon-kah-mah]: a style of manga that more closely resembles Western comic strips.

← Analyzing Media Elements

Reflect on how media elements are combined to enhance meaning. How are the elements of manga combined in this cartoon to enhance its meaning?

Reflecting

Critical Thinking: Think about what you learn about the different styles of manga from reading the definitions. Which style of manga do you think you would prefer? Why?

Metacognition: Reflect on how your ability to analyze media elements is affected by your prior knowledge of, or your interest in, manga.

Media Literacy: Animation is a powerful and increasingly popular form of media with people of various ages. What makes some topics more suitable for animation than others?

MODERN MANGA

A Russian immigrant draws on her passion to become a star in Japanese cartooning.

Newspaper Article by Michele Henry

If the story of her life were a comic strip, Svetlana Chmakova's creative process would span eight to ten panels.

And she'd be a cat trapped in a box in the first frame.

In the second, Svetlana, a comic book author, would stare with wide kitten eyes at the confining walls. The next four panels might show her at various stages of bewilderment, clawing the cardboard and searching for a way out. The seventh panel could depict her stumbling into an exit.

In the eighth, she'd climb through.

"That's the 'Aha!' moment," Svetlana says. "Maybe there would be two more panels … like when the cat gets out and is all happy, then realizes there's another, bigger box. 'Oh no! there's a lot more to get through before the end.'"

When Svetlana, 27, creates manga novels, Japanese-style comic books, there's a lot of stumbling and many 'Aha!' moments. But she accepts that triumphs go hand in hand with frustration. It's part of her passion. And part of what's made this Russian immigrant, who lives in Waterloo, Ontario, a rising star in Japanese cartooning.

"My heart was beating so hard, I was so absorbed in it," she says. "I tried to make my own stories recreate that feeling in myself."

Svetlana, who immigrated to Canada in 1995 and trained at Sheridan College, is almost through her third graphic novel in a short series called *Dramacon*—the first two volumes were published by Tokyopop, a California-based publishing house, in five languages and sold worldwide.

She's written a comic strip for *CosmoGirl* magazine and just inked a deal with YenPress, the manga/graphic novel imprint of one of the largest publishing houses in the world, for a second series called *Nightschool*. In the coming weeks she'll find out whether a Teletoon show she's helped co-create will get the green light. Meanwhile, plans are in the works for her to give manga-drawing workshops at Max the Mutt Animation School, in Toronto, for teens and adults. Not bad for someone who was tired of animation after college and didn't know exactly what she was going to do.

Svetlana freelanced here and there after graduation, and fed her manga passion in her spare time. Bitten by the comic bug while a youngster in Russia, Svetlana fell in love with any cartoon book she could get her hands on. But it was the Russian translation of a manga-influenced book called *ElfQuest*, which she read in 1993, that set her mind on fire.

"My heart was beating so hard, I was so absorbed in it," she says. "I tried to make my own stories recreate that feeling in myself."

Ever since, she's dreamed in story panels. Comics she created and posted online a couple of years ago caught Tokyopop's attention.

Svetlana's first novel, *Dramacon* Volume 1, was nominated for several awards, including the Harvey Award, a North American comic book honour, and it was on the 2005 *Publisher's Weekly* list of best comics. It also won the Mangacast Yomi Award for best global manga 2006. It detailed the exploits of an American manga writer.

"I was very surprised," Svetlana says of her awards. "I wrote it as a fluff piece but I did get deep into characters and tried to be profound."

It worked—partly because of manga's visual vocabulary, she says, which includes all types of symbols, such as a popping vein to signify anger or hearts to convey love. "It's so flexible," she says. "It's full of beauty and expression."

Svetlana is working on her third graphic novel in the *Dramacon* series

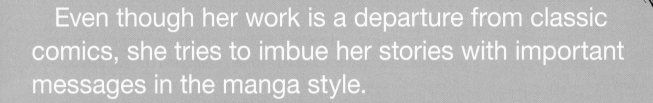

Even though her work is a departure from classic comics, she tries to imbue her stories with important messages in the manga style.

Panels don't need to be in a straight line. The focus in manga literature is on characters and facial expression, Svetlana says. That's why she's fallen in love with the medium and why it's such a hit with kids, she says. Her books are aimed at those aged 13 and over. Traditional superhero cartoons, such as *Superman* or *Spider-Man*, she says, put too much attention on extraneous detail, such as background art. And they might be too steeped in back story for the current generation to grab onto.

Svetlana takes the success of her art seriously. Even though her work is a departure from classic comics, she tries to imbue her stories with important messages in the manga style.

"It's a fact of life," she says. "I want to write books that talk about things … [that] don't preach, but leave question marks that … start conversations. I want to make the world a better place one graphic at a time."

Reflecting

Analyzing Media: What are the elements of newspaper articles used in this selection? How effectively do these elements work together?

Metacognition: How does hearing about someone else's experience help you to think about a career that might be of interest to you?

Media Literacy: Manga uses symbols to share complex ideas quickly. What other media forms use symbols to communicate their message?

Cause and Effect

Cause-and-effect text pattern explains why things happen. Cause-and-effect text pattern is used in many nonfiction books, speeches, and opinion essays—anywhere that the writer is explaining the reason or reasons that something happens.

The *cause* is what happens first, and the *effect* is what happens as a result of the cause. One cause can have more than one effect. One effect can have more than one cause.

Sometimes that one effect may cause another effect, in a chain of effects. For example, the following chain shows the outline for a personal anecdote.

Cause		Effect
	Effect	
	Effect	
	Effect	

Cause	
Cause	Effect
Cause	

My bike was stolen. ⟩ That's why I was late for school. ⟩ As a result, I missed my math test. ⟩ So I had to stay after school.

Key phrases are really important in cause-and-effect text pattern because they help the reader to follow the writer's logic. Here are some of the key phrases you might see or use:

If … then	So that	Because
As a result	Since	Therefore
That's why		

Transfer Your Learning

Across the Strands

Oral Language: When you're listening to a speech, listen for key words that let you know it's using cause-and-effect text pattern. How can doing so help you follow the speaker's logic?

Across the Curriculum

Science: Opinion essays on environmental issues, such as global warming, often use cause-and-effect text pattern. Why is cause-and-effect text pattern a good choice for writing intended to persuade us?

Talk About It
In your opinion, can animals communicate with humans?

CONVERSATIONS WITH GREAT APES

Nonfiction Article by Margery Facklam

Cause-and-Effect Text Pattern →

Cause-and-effect text pattern explains why things happen. What 'why' question might be answered in this nonfiction article?

Cause-and-Effect Text Pattern ↘

The cause happens first, and the effect happens as a result of the cause. What is the cause in this sentence? What is the effect?

Washoe, a chimpanzee, was the first animal to point to herself and say, "I." Scientists had argued for centuries about whether or not animals knew who they were.

Washoe grew up in Allen and Beatrice Gardner's backyard. In 1966, the Gardners began to teach the young chimp American Sign Language, which is used by many deaf people. It is not English but rather a combination of gestures and hand motions.

At first Washoe made simple signs, such as those for *hat, out, come,* and *ball.* A lot of scientists thought that wasn't so amazing, because she was just imitating her trainers. But all baby animals learn by imitation. Human babies certainly do. We hold up a ball and say to the baby, "Ball." Pretty soon the baby learns to call that round thing a *ball.* By the time she was five years old, Washoe knew 150 signs. She could tell the Gardners, "You me go out," for example. She knew the difference between "You tickle me" and "I tickle you." She loved to be tickled.

Once in a while Washoe invented signs. Before she ate, Washoe had to put on a bib. The gesture the Gardners used for the word *bib* was the gesture for *wiper.* Washoe was supposed to touch her mouth with five fingers in a wiping motion. But Washoe forgot, so instead she drew the outline of a bib on her chest.

Cause-and-Effect
Text Pattern

→

One cause can have more than
one effect. If the cause is not
knowing the names of things,
what are the effects?

Cause-and-Effect
Text Pattern

→

One effect can have more
than one cause. If the effect is
surprising people, what are the
causes? (Notice that the effect
may be listed before the cause,
as it is here.)

Lucy is another chimpanzee who learned to "talk" to humans in American Sign Language. When she didn't know the names for what she saw, she used combinations of words she did know. She called swans *water birds*; watermelon was *candy drink*.

Koko is a gorilla who did the same thing. She called a mask an *eye hat* and a ring a *finger bracelet*. A frozen banana was a *fruit lollipop*, and a lemon was a *dirty orange*. *Dirty* was Koko's word for anything she didn't like, and she didn't like lemons.

Of all the great apes that have learned sign, Koko is the most famous. She was the first animal to tell us how she felt. She really surprised everyone when she made jokes, rhymed words, and insulted people. Koko was born in 1971, and a year later she went to live with Dr. Francine (Penny) Patterson.

Some scientists weren't sure that Koko really knew what she was doing. But when one scientist asked Koko in sign language if she was a person or a gorilla, Koko signed back, "Fine animal gorilla."

Koko has always loved to have someone read to her. She still spends hours looking at picture books, especially *The Three Little Kittens* and *Puss in Boots*. She makes the sign for cat by drawing two fingers across her cheek like whiskers.

Before Koko's birthday one year, someone showed her three real kittens. Koko looked them over carefully and finally chose one that had no tail. "Love that," Koko signed. And she named the kitten All Ball.

Koko with Francine Patterson

Dr. Patterson drew a picture of a cat on Koko's birthday cake. She asked Koko, "What did I draw?" Koko signed, "Ball. Koko love visit Ball." Koko acted like a child with a pet. She would never hurt the kitten. If All Ball nipped her, Koko would sign, "Obnoxious." Then later she'd sign, "Soft good cat cat." Koko carried All Ball on her back the way a gorilla mother carries her baby.

↙ **Cause-and-Effect Text Pattern**

Sometimes one effect may cause another effect, in a chain of effects. What is the chain of effects here?

A gorilla in a zoo in the United Kingdom communicates with visitors.

Scientists continue to ask, "What is language?" and "Do apes really talk?" Of course, Koko and Washoe and Lucy and the others don't use our language because no matter how hard they try, chimpanzees and gorillas can never talk as we do. They don't have the same kind of vocal cords. But does that matter? They speak to us in their own way. For the first time, there is real communication between humans and other animals. It's a wonderful gift.

What more would they ask us if they could? What more would they tell us if they could?

← **Cause-and-Effect Text Pattern**

Key phrases (such as *if … then*, *so that*, or *because*) signal cause-and-effect relationships. What word or phrase in this section indicates a cause-and-effect relationship?

Reflecting

Metacognition: How did thinking about the characteristics of cause-and-effect text pattern as you read help you follow the author's argument?

Synthesizing: Use your understanding of how you learned language to help you understand this selection. How does thinking about your own experiences affect your understanding of the selection?

Critical Literacy: Was the author successful in convincing you that great apes are able to communicate with humans? Should she have included more information to support the other side of the argument?

Talk About It
Do you always believe everything you read?

Beware of Bad Science

Article by Diane Swanson

One day soon, if it hasn't happened already, you'll realize you've been terribly misled. Like everyone else, you've likely made some important decisions that were based on bad science—or the bad reporting of good science. Suppose, for instance, that you bought a bottle of Dr. Smart's Cough Syrup for Grandpa without realizing that Dr. Smart did her research only on poodles, not people. What if you decided to abandon your dream of becoming a teacher because an analysis of your handwriting claimed you didn't have what it takes? Imagine you'd sworn off your favourite soft drink, Silly Soda, because a news reporter announced it can make you sick—only the reporter failed to mention you'd have to drink 40 glasses a day to feel any ill effects. Arghhh! You've been led down the garden path—three times!

How? Well, you can't assume that whatever might clear your pet poodle's throat is going to help Grandpa. After all, there are important differences between dogs and people. And a handwriting analysis is much like a fortune cookie. It's fun to see what it has to say, but you wouldn't want to plan your life—or your career—around it. As for Silly Soda, think about it. Every day, you eat food that could be harmful if you overdid it. Take salt, for instance. Small quantities help you contract your muscles, but too much might raise your blood pressure, bring on kidney stones, or trigger some heavy-duty headaches. Just because downing large amounts of something is unsafe doesn't mean that eating small amounts is necessarily bad for you.

What do you stand to lose if you don't sift out the bad science—and the bad reporting of good science—that's hidden among all the good stuff? The sky's the limit because science affects every part of your life. It influences what you eat and drink. It determines what kind of house you live in, what type of bike you ride, and how fast you can reach your friends on the Internet. It affects how you're treated when you're sick or injured, from the simple bandage you slap on a cut to the miniature video camera you may one day swallow in a pill to get the inside scoop on your ailing intestines.

Imagine what happens when inadequate, faulty, or phony science creeps into your life. It's used incorrectly to declare products "safe" or "unsafe." It persuades you to buy goods that are trash. It promotes poor medical treatments that don't help and discourages you from getting care that does. In court, it's used to back up unreliable—even false—claims. For instance, doctors have given "expert" testimony supporting people who claimed their cancer was caused by a blow from a can of orange juice or the handle of an umbrella.

Some lobby groups present bad science to sway public opinion. One famous example concerned Alar, a product that used to be sprayed on apples to keep them fresh. By the 1980s, scientists had some concern that very high doses of Alar might cause cancer in test animals. In 1989, a lobby group that was pushing to have Alar banned in the United States released the results of a single, poorly done study to the hosts of a TV news show called *60 Minutes*. Although the animals used in the study had been exposed to amounts of Alar 266 000 times greater than people would ever be, the researchers concluded Alar threatened human lives—especially the lives of small children.

When *60 Minutes* featured this study, people panicked. Families and businesses pitched out their apples and apple juice, and pressed the American government to ban Alar. Even though government environmental and food agencies announced that the small amounts of Alar on apples were harmless, the public insisted Alar should go. It was withdrawn from use later that year. Whether or not it should have been will probably never be known. The point is that it was withdrawn for the wrong reason—limited, faulty research.

With all that's affected by science, it's lucky that people like you are willing to sort the good from the bad. Although it might seem like a big role to take on, you don't have to be a rocket scientist—or any other kind of scientist—to succeed. Mostly, you just have to be willing to ask questions and think clearly.

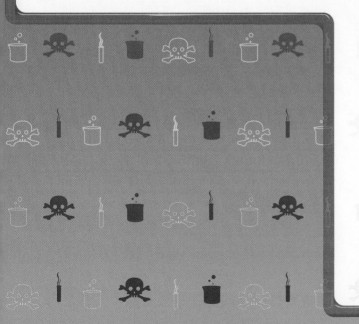

Beware of Bad Science

Media Watch!

Always Ask

1. Gather just half the facts and you have just half the story. Always ask: Were the data complete?

2. Good researchers present their results clearly and completely, and demonstrate how they draw their conclusions. Always ask: Were the results abused to force a conclusion?

3. It's your right to know more about the science that affects you, your health, and your lifestyle. You need to know how well you can rely on the research behind it. Always ask: Was the research reported adequately?

4. Consider how times have changed. With today's communications technology, a single news report can circle the globe almost instantly, reaching millions of people. Be on the alert. Always ask: Did the reporter get all the facts?

5. Reporters usually only have a minute or two behind a microphone—or a single column in a newspaper—and they can't possibly do a thorough job of presenting a scientific study. Always ask: Was the research reported adequately?

6. Even facts that are well researched and accurately reported can mislead the public if they're not explained well. Putting research into a bigger picture, or context, also helps people understand it better. Always ask: Was the research explained well?

Mind Watch

Popular Perception

Everybody says the number of spots on a ladybug indicates its age, so it must be true. Friday's rock concert is sure to sell out because so many kids want to attend. You can't go wrong with cough syrup—everybody finds it helps cure a cough.

Each of these statements uses popularity as the reason for claiming that it's true. But popularity is relevant in only one of them—the second statement. The reasoning in the other two is faulty. The relationship between a ladybug's spots and its age is common folklore, but that doesn't make it true. Most ladybugs have all their spots within 12 hours of becoming adults. And just because many people believe in the value of cough syrup doesn't mean it actually cures their coughing. "Everybody" thinking something doesn't make it right. Nor does the fact that something is unpopular make it wrong. Watch out for this kind of faulty reasoning.

Always think: Do I think a statement is true just because many people do, or do I check out the facts with scientific sources?

For hundreds of years, people the world over believed the Earth was flat—but that didn't make it right.

Winning Strategies

Discover How Science Works

Become familiar with the general approach to scientific research. All fields follow the same basic pattern of investigation, so if you get "up close and personal" with one field, you'll feel more at home with the others. Read widely, visit science labs, take part in experiments at hands-on science museums, attend open houses at universities and government science departments, and talk to scientists and science educators.

Strengthen your sense of analysis by learning a bit about statistics, too. You'll not only improve your understanding of statistics, but you'll realize how easily statistics can be used to mislead you.

It helps to get as many facts and views as possible. Look for balanced, complete, and accurate coverage.

Sharpen Your Thinking Skills

Honing your mind is not something you should work at just now and then. Make mental fitness—like physical fitness—a part of your daily routine. Keep working to sift evidence from propaganda, logic from superstition, conclusions from assumptions, and science from folklore. Your powers of critical thinking need plenty of exercise, but the workouts can be fun as well as useful. Pick up some books or software programs that offer brain bafflers, mind teasers, and logic puzzles. Enjoy.

Reflecting

Analyzing Text Patterns: What causes and effects are explored in this selection? What 'why' question does the text answer?

Metacognition: It is important to think critically and use metacognitive skills when learning a new topic. What metacognitive skills are mentioned in this article?

Synthesizing: Think about the advice this article gives, and media texts you've enjoyed. How important is the information in this article to you? If you could reduce everything you learned from this article to one simple piece of advice, what would it be?

History

The reading strategy you learned in this unit can help you understand text in other subject areas. As you read, combine your prior knowledge with what you are learning to synthesize the information in this text.

Black Loyalists

One group of loyalists was former slaves from the Thirteen Colonies. Slavery was legal in all North American colonies until the mid-nineteenth century.

Slaves owned by rebels had been promised freedom if they helped the British. When the American Revolution ended, approximately 3000 Black Loyalists came north to Nova Scotia.

The first goal of the Black Loyalists, like all Loyalists, was to build shelter. However, tools and nails were in short supply everywhere. Black Loyalists were usually the last to receive supplies, such as cut lumber, from the British.

A Black Wood Cutter at Shelburne, Nova Scotia, by W. Booth, 1788

Many descendants of Black Loyalists still live in Nova Scotia. Here Elizabeth Cromwell, past president of the Black Loyalist Heritage Association, walks with former Governor General Adrienne Clarkson outside the Black Loyalist Old School Museum in Birchtown, Nova Scotia.

William Dyott's Diary, October 1788

[We] walked through the woods about two miles [3.2 kilometres] from the barracks to a Black Loyalist town called Birch Town. At the evacuation of New York there were a great number of these poor people given lands and settled here—The place is beyond description wretched [terrible], situated on the coast in the middle of barren rocks, and partly surrounded by a thick impenetrable [dark] wood—Their huts miserable to guard against the inclemency [harshness] of a Nova Scotia winter, and their existence almost depending on what they could lay up [store] in summer. I think I never saw wretchedness and poverty so strongly perceptible [obvious] in the garb [clothing] and the countenance [facial expression] of the human species as in these miserable outcasts.

Thomas Peters and the Sierra Leone Company

Thomas Peters and many other members of the Black Pioneers went to Nova Scotia at the end of the American Revolution. By 1791, many Black Loyalists were still having trouble getting farms. At most, they received less than half a hectare each. In contrast, other Loyalists received hundreds of hectares.

Peters wrote many petitions on behalf of Black Loyalists. When these were rejected, he travelled to England to present them to the Crown. Even this plea was rejected. However, while in London, Peters caught the attention of the Sierra Leone Company. The company was run by abolitionists, people who campaigned to end slavery. The Sierra Leone Company was trying to establish a settlement for freed slaves in Sierra Leone, Africa.

Peters and the other Black Loyalists had few alternatives. They could accept the poor land allotted to them in Nova Scotia. They could serve with the British army in the West Indies. Many chose to accept the offer of land and free transportation to Sierra Leone. They called it the "Province of Freedom."

Peters convinced 1100 people to go to Sierra Leone in January 1792. When they arrived in Africa, conditions were not much better than what they had left behind. They experienced poor weather, difficult relationships with local Africans, and delays in receiving land grants. Their settlement—Freetown—struggled with problems for many years. However, in the nineteenth century, Black Loyalists became an elite group in Sierra Leone. Most of those who had stayed in Nova Scotia remained on the margins of society for many more decades.

Reflecting

Synthesizing: Which parts of this text helped you gain a new perspective or ideas on the topic?

Metacognition: To understand a period in history, which do you find it's most helpful to do:

• read actual historical documents like diaries and letters?

• read facts about the period?

• examine images from the period?

• or a combination of these?

Make an Impression

What events or people have made an impression on you?

Unit Learning Goals

- evaluate texts while reading
- choose appropriate writing conventions

- communicate effectively
- create DVD covers

- analyze problem/ solution text pattern

Transfer Your Learning: The Arts

How to → Evaluate Texts

After seeing a movie, you may tell a friend that you liked or disliked it. To express your opinion, you evaluate the movie's strengths and weaknesses, its message and viewpoints.

You evaluate what you *read* by questioning the text.

- Think about what you already know or feel about the subject.
- Reflect on whether the text makes sense. Decide whether the author has written in a way that is convincing.
- Reflect on your response to how the text is organized.
- Decide whether you agree or disagree with the author's message or point of view. Your evaluation should be based on a careful reading of the text, with evidence to support your final opinion or judgment.

For Narrative Texts, Ask Yourself	For Informational Texts, Ask Yourself
• Are the characters believable? • Is the text organized effectively so that events make sense? • What is the text's message or point of view? • What do the characters or author seem to believe or value? What clues tell me so? • How do I feel about those beliefs or values?	• Is the information accurate or, if the subject is unfamiliar, does it appear to be accurate? Is the source reliable? • Is the text organized effectively for the topic? • Is the writer's main point or argument reasonable? • What is the text's message or point of view? • What does the author or the people featured in the text seem to believe or value? What clues tell me so? • How do I feel about those beliefs or values?

Transfer Your Learning

Across the Strands

Media Literacy: Think about a movie you have recommended to others recently. What aspects of the movie made you give it a positive review?

Across the Curriculum

The Arts: If you were evaluating a work of art, such as a painting or sculpture, how would you change the questions in the chart?

Talk About It

What do you first notice about a person? What do you want people to first notice about you?

In the Blink Eye of an

Evaluating   →   ## Profiling Malcolm Gladwell's book *Blink*

Article by Erise Kara

Evaluating

When evaluating, decide first whether a text is narrative or informational so you know what questions to ask. How can you tell that this selection is informational?

What gives us our first impressions? We meet new people or see new things, and form quick first impressions. We depend on those first impressions to get us through our day. Most of these first impressions are made very quickly, and most of them serve us well. How can that be when we are making them so fast?

In his bestselling book *Blink*, author Malcolm Gladwell tells us we should imagine that our brains each contain a giant computer. That computer, called the *adaptive unconscious*, helps us to survive by making quick decisions. If we step out in the middle of the street and a truck is coming at us fast, we don't stand still and weigh our options. We move instantly to get out of harm's way.

Evaluating

Think about what you already know or feel about the subject. How does Gladwell's theory fit with what you already think or know about forming first impressions?

Gladwell calls the formation of these first impressions *thin-slicing*. When we thin-slice, we "sift through the situation in front of us, throwing out all that is irrelevant while we zero in on what really matters."

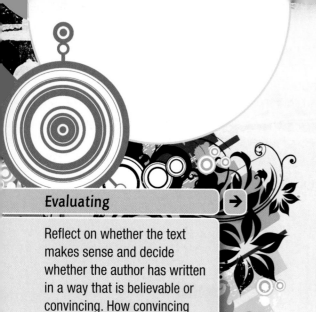

Think about what you notice when you meet someone for the first time. Maybe that girl is wearing a T-shirt of your favourite band. That's relevant to you, and you'll make judgments based on that shirt. Another person might notice the skateboard she's carrying because that's what's relevant to him. That's thin-slicing.

Before you meet a new person, let's imagine you have a chance to look in his/her school locker. In the locker you find a soccer ball, a binder covered with rock-band stickers, the latest issue of *Sports Illustrated* magazine, and one worn running shoe nestled between a half-eaten sandwich and a math book. What first impression could thin-slicing give you of this person?

If your answer is someone who is athletic, active, and interested in music, you made some inferences from what you observed. These inferences allowed you to come to some reasonable conclusions. If you are also convinced you know the gender of the person, you are probably jumping to a conclusion that cannot be proved by the little bit of information that came from the locker.

Gladwell says that we can teach ourselves to do a better job of thin-slicing by training our minds to focus only on the most relevant facts and learning how to control our first impressions.

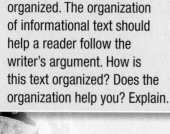

Evaluating →

Reflect on whether the text makes sense and decide whether the author has written in a way that is believable or convincing. How convincing is Gladwell's argument as presented in this example?

Evaluating →

Reflect on how the text is organized. The organization of informational text should help a reader follow the writer's argument. How is this text organized? Does the organization help you? Explain.

Malcolm Gladwell is a writer from Elmira, Ontario, who has written several best-selling nonfiction books. Looking at this photo, what are your first impressions of Malcolm?

Thin-Slicing: The Backpack Experiment

Here are photos of three people's backpacks. What are your first impressions of these people, based on their backpacks?

← **Evaluating**

Decide whether you agree or disagree with the author's message or point of view. Does the backpack experiment help convince you of Gladwell's argument? What evidence supports your opinion?

Evaluating

A graphic organizer like this one can help you organize your thoughts as you evaluate a text.

Questions I Asked of the Text	Answers or Clues in the Text	My Final Opinion or Judgment

Reflecting

Evaluating: What is your judgment on this article? Does the article successfully convince you of Gladwell's argument? Why or why not?

Metacognition: Did your thoughts about first impressions change as you read this article? Explain.

Critical Literacy: Compare and contrast Gladwell's values and beliefs with your own values and beliefs. What would you like to ask Gladwell to help you clarify your thoughts?

Talk About It

When does staying in the background pay off?

How to Fly Under the Radar

Nonfiction article by John Saade and Joe Borgenicht

Do you watch reality TV shows? Have you noticed how often the winning contestants are the ones who make the biggest impression on others? Another way to win is known as "flying under the radar," which means not making an impression. These writers give reality-TV-show wannabes some valuable advice on flying under the radar.

Taking the quiet path toward victory can be just as successful in manipulating the team as being the alpha dog. Lurking in the background can be an excellent position from which to observe other contestants and gather evidence while remaining safely out of the line of fire.

Masters of How to Fly Under the Radar stay in the game until the very end—when no one has even given them a second glance, because their threat factor is zero. Others will dip in and out, switching between playing the role of the quiet, supportive benchwarmer and the vocal team leader.

Here's some advice on how to stay on the sidelines all the way to the final round. But be careful—management trainer Suzanne Gooler notes that if your allies begin to question your ability, it's time to step up and prove yourself.

1. Do just enough to avoid causing problems.

2. If you have chores, quietly go about your business. Let others complain about the work, the leaders, or the players who sleep all day.

This image is from *Survivor, Season 4*. This was the only season where the final three contestants were women.

3. Be agreeable.

4. Let others make the decisions, even if you have a conflicting opinion. Do it their way to show that you are still useful.

In *The Apprentice* it's usually the leader of the losing team that's fired. He/she is held responsible for all bad decisions.

How to Fly Under the Radar

5. Avoid letting others into your personal life.

6. Do not discuss your homesickness or your family or friends. If others want to talk, listen, but add just enough of your own information to avoid appearing aloof or uncaring.

7. Be as physically unassuming as possible. Hunch your shoulders, avoid making eye contact, sit down when people talk to you, and retreat to the back of the line during group activities.

Take a careful look at this photo from *Survivor*. Which contestant looks the most physically unassuming?

8. Take a safe, neutral position during arguments in the house or camp.

9. Allow others to passionately attempt to resolve issues or raise their voices to make a point. Remain disengaged, and go with the flow.

All of these strategies will silently communicate to others that you are not a threat, which will certainly work to your advantage as they vote off stronger or more opinionated characters.

In shows like this one—*Eco-Challenge*—teams have to work together to succeed. Which of the strategies for flying under the radar would it still be smart to follow?

Reflecting

Evaluating: What opinion or judgment have you formed about this article? Do you agree or disagree with the authors' message or point of view? What evidence supports your opinion?

Metacognition: What comprehension strategies work best for you when you read unfamiliar expressions, such as *alpha dog*, *benchwarmer*, or *threat factor*?

Media Literacy: Think about reality TV shows you've watched. What types of contestants are not reflected in this article? Can every contestant be placed in a specific category? Create a chart showing the different types of contestants and their characteristics.

Talk About It
Sometimes simple events can leave a major impression.

The Moose

Personal Anecdote by Glen Cooper

I have a story to tell about my father and the situation that occurred when he killed a moose early in April. I remember this very vividly because it struck me very hard and personally. This was the first time that I ever realized the direct impact that the hydro-electric development and the massive environmental destruction had on me.

I went out to visit my parents in the woods. Early that day my father went moose hunting. He was gone all day. Usually he comes home around 5:00 p.m., when the sun begins to set. That evening he came home at about 9:30 p.m. Everybody was gone. My brother Alan and I were the only ones there. My father walked through the door, totally silent and didn't say anything.

I was standing in the kitchen and I asked him if he had killed a moose. He did not respond to my question right away. We could tell my Dad was hurt. He gave my brother a hug and said: "We can't eat it."

This photo shows a sculpture called *The Spirit of Haida Gwaii* by artist Bill Reid. The sculpture can be found in the Canadian Museum of Civilization in Gatineau, Québec. Crowded into this canoe are Raven, Eagle, Bear, Mother, Beaver, Wolf, Mouse Woman, Frog, and others. They fight with one another, but still paddle the canoe forward. Many people feel that this sculpture reflects the struggle of the First Nations people to overcome obstacles. How does this sculpture's message connect with the author's message in "The Moose"?

He said he had killed a moose but as he was cutting it open, he saw that the insides were full of mucous, the pancreas had white spots, the kidneys were very small, and the heart had water on it.

He had tears in his eyes, although he did not cry bitterly. I remember a story I was told which said that an elderly man never cries because he must stay strong for the young.

My father, who is going to be sixty, wept before my eyes because he had killed a moose which he could not feed to his family.

Reflecting

Evaluating: What is this author's message? How do you respond to that message?

Metacognition: What personal experiences or knowledge influence your opinion of this text?

Critical Thinking: The author says that this situation struck him "very hard and personally." Do you think the author gives the reader too little or just enough information to understand the situation and his response? Explain.

Talk About It
What do you notice most about the people you care about?

Now I See YOU

Poem by Maxine Tynes

(poem for my mother, Ada Maxwell Tynes)

When did I start looking at you, my mother?
I don't know;
but often, it's your hands I'll watch
all brown, and bumpy-smooth
those same hands that
held and cradled me,
in my new life.

I look at your nose,
so high and strong, for a Black woman;
the same nose of
some noble African tribe. But where? Where?

I look at your eyes.
They've seen so much. So much.
You'll never tell me.

The hardest look of all
was the one I took of you sleeping.
and, missing my dad, still;
you lie with pillows piled high
and nestled close beside you, in sleep.

A Moment of Reflection
by Neville Clarke

Neville Clarke met model Karen Eyo in drawing class. During one modelling session, Karen was quiet and close to tears. She confided that she felt her life was not on track. Neville was compelled to capture her despair on canvas. Karen went on to publish a book of poems based on the experience. This painting has made Neville a recognized figure in Canadian art.

Reflecting

Evaluating: What does the poet value and believe? The artist? Compare these values and beliefs with your own.

Metacognition: Which do you find it easier to evaluate, the poem or the painting? Why do you think that is?

Critical Literacy: How does the poet want you to respond to the two women she describes in her poem—her mother and herself? How does the artist want you to respond to the woman in the painting?

FAMILY SKETCHES

Poem by Fred Wah

my father hurt-
ing at the table
sitting hurting
at suppertime
deep inside very
far down inside
because I can't stand the ginger
in the beef and greens
he cooked for us tonight
and years later tonight
that look on his face
appears now on mine
my children
my food
their food
my father
their father
me mine
the father
very far
very very far
inside

全家福

Tian Li, *Fruit on Table*

Reflecting

Evaluating: In your opinion, does this poem effectively express the poet's feelings? Support your answer.

Metacognition: What strategies do you use to make sense of and evaluate this poem? What strategies do you use to make sense of and evaluate the painting?

Critical Thinking: How does your personal experience at family meals help you to evaluate this poem?

How to ➤ Use Writing Conventions

Next time you write something, analyze any errors.

• Did you know the correct convention but were too concerned with content to notice your mistake? Those errors can be easily fixed when you edit your text.

• Did you not know you'd made a mistake until someone pointed it out? Those errors show you are growing as a writer and are willing to take risks.

Editing Symbols

Symbol	What It Means
ℒ	Take this out.
∧	Add a word or letter.
≡	Capitalize this letter.
/	Make this letter lowercase.
⊙	Add a period.
⌄	Add a comma.
∨	Add an apostrophe.
#	Put in a space.

It doesn't matter what kind of writing you're doing—a note to your sister, a text message to a friend, or a history essay—all writing communicates meaning.

You probably find that family and friends understand even your most cryptic notes: "Gone 2 mall w J.B. & Vi. CU." If you are writing for other people, use standard English conventions so your ideas will be understood.

What are those writing conventions? They're the rules of grammar, punctuation, and spelling that help readers understand and focus on your message. Errors in the conventions can confuse and distract readers.

These are just *some* of the conventions you will want to use.

• Divide text into logical paragraphs.

• Use appropriate punctuation marks (periods, commas, semicolons, and so on).

• Make subjects and verbs agree.

• Spell each word correctly.

Use or play with standard writing conventions to enhance your message or voice. For example, if you're writing an article about text messaging, you'll probably use some of the short forms acceptable in that format.

Transfer Your Learning

Across the Strands

Media Literacy: Products, stores, and ads sometimes play with writing conventions, for example, the major toy store chain Toys "Я" Us. How does this approach help the creators reach their intended audience?

Across the Curriculum

The Arts: Scripts for dramatic productions need to pay attention to writing conventions. Why does it matter that scripts use the appropriate punctuation?

Talk About It
What makes text messaging so popular?

Talk to Me
Text Messaging Takes Off

Newspaper Article by Erin Anderssen

In the Bowmanville, Ontario, theatre, with the romantic storyline rolling out before him, Matthew did what any restless teenager with free fingers would do: he hauled out his cellphone and started typing. Two rows ahead, Nikola got pinged on her phone. Five seats over, Kevin received the same text message on his. The rest of the audience moved on to a fight scene.

Writing Conventions ➔

Choice of conventions depends on your audience. Why is the use of short forms appropriate in this text message?

DO U FIND THS BORIN?

Turns out, they did. By the end of the movie, Matthew was up to speed on the major homework assignments his friends were facing, the events of their day (WHT HAV U BEEN DOIN?), and whether there was any fresh gossip at their school. N2M, they typed, or "not too much."

Even better, he had his Saturday night planned: an evening at Nikola's if she was allowed to have SUM FRIENDS OVER. Otherwise, they'd GO2 MALL. Said Matthew: "It was a really slow movie."

Writing Conventions ➔

If you are writing for a wider audience, use standard English conventions so your ideas will be understood. Why are short forms only appearing as examples in this newspaper article? Why are translations of some short forms provided?

Matthew, 15, qualifies as a text junkie; he sends up to 30 messages a day on his cellphone, from the bus, in class ("when you don't have to pay attention," he insists), and sometimes at the movies. He knows the vowel-starved spelling rules, and he can write sentences almost at the speed it takes to type on a keyboard.

Writing Conventions →

Use the rules of grammar, punctuation, and spelling to help readers understand and focus on the message. Note how this author uses a semicolon to help the reader understand how ideas are linked.

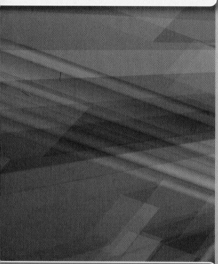

Writing Conventions →

Short forms allow friends to develop a shared language. What is the disadvantage of trying to use this form of communication with a wider audience?

In the under-20 crowd, text messaging is used to arrange secret meetings in the washroom, to organize lunch dates, to swarm hot sales at the mall, and to flirt. It is the modern version of passing notes, with the clear advantage of not having to be anywhere near the person you're passing to. This is the thrill, the ability to have a covert conversation—sometimes practical, usually frivolous—when you aren't supposed to be conversing.

Teenagers are way out in front on the texting circuit, and loyal users of its close computer cousin, instant messaging, which mimics a real-time conversation better than e-mail. Instant messaging sends alerts when your friends log on to their computers and the rapid chat that bounces back and forth uses many of the same text-messaging abbreviations. It has replaced the hours that teenagers of old once spent on the phone; 16-year-old Kaitie in London, Ontario, says she uses it at least two hours every night. MSN Messenger, for instance, now has more than 14 million users in Canada.

This is a generation that is used to being connected all the time, that has no concept of not being able to reach someone, and whose parents are often forking over the cash to keep them linked—what one phone company calls "the wireless allowance." (Depending on your phone plan, text messages cost about 10 cents apiece to send, but have no long-distance charges.)

Fourteen-year-old Katrina of Langley, British Columbia, has trouble even imagining a world before cellphones and instant messaging; she is horrified at the thought of her parents' disconnected state when they were young. "They didn't have cellphones, did they?" she asks. "What if you really needed to talk to somebody?"

Teenagers have harnessed texting's power to organize: In Britain, for instance, Prince William is plagued by hordes of text-messaging teenagers who track his every move. And they are fluent in its informal language, which allows them to develop secret codes among their friends.

The pop culture references abound: Tolkien fans are reportedly known for greeting each other with 1O2RULALL. (Which, as everyone who's seen the movies knows, means "One Ring to rule them all.")

Mostly, they're using the now-familiar standards: LOL for laughing out loud, L8 for late, NP for no problem, and peppering it with emoticons (try :-D, for laughing) to give feeling to their messages. It is habit-forming: Haley, 14, of Toronto, has to regularly reread her school papers and fix all the U's and R's. "I do it without thinking," she says.

In a study of online language conducted last year by Neil Randall, an English professor at the University of Waterloo, 85% of those under 20 said they used it mostly for fun. "Bad news," Dr. Randall says, "does not travel well over the Internet."

While nobody watches their own grammar when messaging, e-mail has become a formal form of communication, reserved for teachers and bosses and is more likely to get spell-checked. There's even a certain etiquette developing around "away" messages, the notes that people post with their instant message providers to let friends know that they're logged on but not available.

There's a debate now about whether all this short-form, high-speed writing is dulling the brains of the text generation. Dr. Naomi Baron, who studies Internet use and its effect on language, wonders if we're losing our ability to "pause and ponder" in writing. "Not that abbreviations are a problem," she says. "Not that spelling is sacred. The question is: Are we thinking clearly?"

Dr. Randall thinks this is nonsense. He says teenagers are simply adapting writing so it can move at "breakneck speeds."

Writing Conventions

Use or play with conventions to enhance your message or voice. How do text messagers play with conventions?

1O2RULALL

Reflecting

Reading Like a Writer: What can you learn from this author about how to use standard writing conventions? Was there anything the author did, related to the use of writing conventions, that surprised you?

Metacognition: What short forms and symbols do you use when you are taking notes? How do these help you to organize your thoughts and learn new ideas more efficiently or effectively?

Critical Literacy: What is the author's opinion or viewpoint on text messaging? How do you know?

Talk About It

In what situation do you leave people with the best impression: When you speak with them face to face? When you talk over the phone? When you text message? Why do you think that is?

TXTS

Poem by Andrew Wilson

We're not quite tuned
to each other's English
need to read faces
so 2 make d8s
we txt not fone:
written words
2 b sure we're understood.

Reflecting

Reading Like a Writer: How does this poem play with conventions? Is the poem effective at delivering its message?

Critical Thinking: How does the title help the reader understand what the selection will be about?

Talk About It
What sort of impression do you make when you use txt language?

Txt Impressions

Glossary by Ken Krepinsky

Txt-ing is taking our language conventions into a whole new age. Don't know how to txt yet? Trying to impress others with your grasp of txt-ing? Here are some of the basics.

Single letters can replace words.
▶ *be* becomes *b*
▶ *see* becomes *c*
▶ *are* becomes *r*
▶ *you* becomes *u*
▶ *why* becomes *y*
▶ *in* becomes *n*

Single digits can replace words.
▶ *ate* becomes *8*
▶ *for* becomes *4*
▶ *to* or *too* becomes *2*
▶ *won* becomes *1*

Other ways to shorten messages?
▶ Vowels are removed. For example, *between* becomes *btwn* and *homework* becomes *hmwk*.
▶ Whole words may be omitted, especially words like *a* or *the*.
▶ Punctuation is generally removed; only question marks and exclamation marks are sometimes used. After a period, the space and capital letter are often left out.
▶ A slash (*/*) indicates an abbreviation, such as *w/* for *with* and *s/t* for *something*.

Reflecting

Reading Like a Writer: How confusing or distracting do you find the use of short forms in text messaging? Do you think all readers feel the same way?

Metacognition: What do you do to help your readers understand the short forms you use? What comprehension strategies help you figure out any unfamiliar short forms?

Critical Literacy: How do you think people who never use text messaging might respond to this selection?

How to ➤ # Communicate Effectively

When you talk about something that matters to you, you want to involve your listeners. You want them to see the situation from your perspective, to feel what you feel, and to want what you want.

1. Make sure you really care about your topic. If you don't care, listeners won't care either.

2. Take responsibility for what you say. Make sure your language is free of prejudice, offensive comments, and bias.

3. Use words that make sense to your audience. For example, not everyone may understand the jargon connected with your favourite hobby.

4. Choose appropriate expression for your topic, purpose, and audience. Expression is made up of seven vocal effects:
   - *volume*, from a whisper to a shout
   - *pitch*, from high to low
   - *rate*, or speed of delivery, including pauses, from quick to slow
   - *duration*, or how slowly or quickly a word or phrase is spoken
   - *tone*, or vocal quality, from nasal to whiny, screechy to raspy
   - *articulation*, or clear pronunciation of words
   - *emphasis*, the stress on syllables, words, or phrases

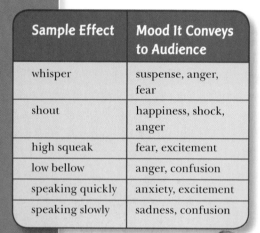

Sample Effect	Mood It Conveys to Audience
whisper	suspense, anger, fear
shout	happiness, shock, anger
high squeak	fear, excitement
low bellow	anger, confusion
speaking quickly	anxiety, excitement
speaking slowly	sadness, confusion

Transfer Your Learning

Across the Strands

Reading: If you are asked to read a text aloud, what vocal effects are you most likely to use? How does the type of text influence your choice of vocal effects?

Across the Curriculum

History: When you speak in history class, what vocal effects do you use to show you feel strongly about the topic?

Talk About It
What is the value of speech?

The Value of Speech

Speech by Helen Keller

Communicating Effectively

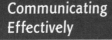

Speakers use different vocal effects so that their expression works with their topic, purpose, and audience. The words you choose to emphasize change the meaning you give to a phrase. What word would you emphasize in this title?

Communicating Effectively

Speakers make sure they really care about their topic, so that their listeners care, too. What words does Helen Keller use that show you she cares passionately about her topic?

Helen Keller was born in 1880 in Alabama. As a baby, Helen suffered a serious illness that left her deaf and blind. With the help of her teacher Anne Sullivan, Helen Keller's world of incomprehension changed to one of communication. Helen went on to become a public speaker. This speech was given at a school for the hearing impaired.

Helen Keller

If you knew all the joy I feel in being able to speak to you today, I think you would have some idea of the value of speech to the deaf, and you would understand why I want every little deaf child in all this great world to have an opportunity to learn to speak.

I know that much has been said and written on this subject, and that there is a wide difference of opinion among teachers of the deaf in regard to oral instruction. It seems very strange to me that there should be this difference of opinion; I cannot understand how anyone interested in our education can fail to appreciate the satisfaction we feel in being able to express our thoughts in living words.

Helen Keller (centre) talks with a group of people on the set of a film.

Communicating Effectively

When speakers talk about something important to them, they need to involve their audience. They should use words that make sense to that audience. How does Helen help her audience understand her passion and feel involved?

Why, I use speech constantly, and I cannot begin to tell you how much pleasure it gives me to do so. Of course I know that it is not always easy for strangers to understand me, but it will be by and by; and in the meantime I have the unspeakable happiness of knowing that my family and friends rejoice in my ability to speak. My little sister and baby brother love to have me tell them stories in the long summer evenings when I am at home; and my mother and teacher often ask me to read to them from my favourite books. I also discuss the political situation with my dear father, and we decide the most perplexing questions quite as satisfactorily to ourselves as if I could see and hear.

So you see what a blessing speech is to me. It brings me into closer and tenderer relationship with those I love, and makes it possible for me to enjoy the sweet companionship of a great many persons from whom I should be entirely cut off if I could not talk.

I can remember the time before I learned to speak, and how I used to struggle to express my thoughts by means of the manual alphabet—how my thoughts used to beat against my fingertips like little birds striving to gain their freedom, until one day Miss Fuller opened wide the prison door and let them escape.

Nevertheless, it seemed to me sometimes that I could never use my speech-wings as ... I should use them; there were so many difficulties in the way, so many discouragements; but I kept on trying, knowing that patience and perseverance would win in the end.

And while I worked, I built the most beautiful air castles, and dreamed dreams, the pleasantest of which was of the time when I should talk like other people, and the thought of the pleasure it would give my mother to hear my voice once more sweetened every effort and made every failure an incentive to try harder next time. So I want to say to those who are trying to learn to speak and those who are teaching them: Be of good cheer. Do not think of today's failures, but of the success that may come tomorrow.

You have set yourselves a difficult task, but you will succeed if you persevere, and you will find a joy in overcoming obstacles—a delight in climbing rugged paths, which you would perhaps never know if you did not sometime slip backward—if the road was always smooth and pleasant. Remember, no effort that we make to attain something beautiful is ever lost. Sometime, somewhere, somehow we shall find that which we seek. We shall speak, yes, and sing, too.

Communicating Effectively

Responsible speakers make sure their language is free of prejudice, offensive comments, and bias. Think about Helen's original audience. How do you think they would have felt listening to her speech?

Communicating Effectively

Speakers use appropriate expression so that their audience understands how they feel. Imagine how Helen might have said this paragraph using different vocal effects. What volume would work best? What tone? What pace?

Reflecting

Communicating Effectively: What clues tell you that this speech was originally written to be spoken aloud? What would have made this speech effective for its original audience?

Metacognition: If you were asked to give a speech to your school, what would you talk about? What topic do you feel most strongly about—positively or negatively?

Media Literacy: When you looked at the two photos in this selection, what did you think about the people portrayed? How did the addition of the photos affect your response to the selection?

Talk About It

Do you have to be rich or powerful to make a lasting impression on others?

GOOD GRIEF

Script by Clark Gesner

LUCY: Linus, do you know what I intend? I intend to be a queen. When I grow up, I'm going to be the biggest queen there ever was, and I'll live in this big palace with a big front lawn, and have lots of beautiful dresses to wear. And when I go out in my coach, all the people …

LINUS: Lucy.

LUCY: … all the people will wave and I will shout at them, and …

LINUS: Lucy, I believe "queen" is an inherited title. *(Lucy is silent.)* Yes, I'm quite sure. A person can only become a queen by being born into a royal family of the correct lineage so that she can assume the throne after the death of the reigning monarch. I can't think of any possible way that you could ever become a queen. *(Lucy is still silent.)* I'm sorry, Lucy, but it's true.

LUCY: *(Silence, and then)* … and in the summertime I will go to my summer palace and I'll wear my crown in swimming and everything, and all the people will cheer and I will shout at them.… *(Her vision pops.)* What do you mean I can't be a queen?

LINUS: It's true.

LUCY: There must be a loophole. This kind of thing always has a loophole. Nobody should be kept from being a queen if she wants to be one. IT'S UNDEMOCRATIC!

LINUS: Good grief.

LUCY: It's usually just a matter of knowing the right people. I'll bet a few pieces of well-placed correspondence and I get to be a queen in no time.

LINUS: I think I'll watch television. *(He returns to the set.)*

LUCY: I know what I'll do. If I can't be queen, then I'll be very rich. I'll work and work until I'm very very rich, and then I will buy myself a queendom.

LINUS: Good grief.

LUCY: Yes, I will buy myself a queendom and then I'll kick out the old queen and take over the whole operation myself. I will be head queen. And when I go out in my coach, all the people will wave, and I will … I will…. *(She has glanced at the TV set and become engrossed.)*

Reflecting

Communicating Effectively: These words were originally spoken by actors in an animated movie. Think about the expression they would use to deliver the lines effectively. What do you think would be the hardest part of delivering Lucy's lines?

Metacognition: What speaking strategies have you used that you would suggest Linus try in order to help him communicate with his sister, Lucy?

Critical Thinking: How does the author effectively show each character's personality?

Talk About It
What do you think is the connection between *effort* and *success*?

REACH FOR THE STARS

Radio Essay by Julie Payette, written for CBC Radio

Canadian astronaut Julie Payette flew on the Space Shuttle *Discovery* in 1999 from May 27 to June 6. During the mission, the crew performed the first manual docking of the Shuttle to the *International Space Station* (ISS). Julie served as a mission specialist, supervised the space walk, and operated the Canadarm robotic arm. She was the first Canadian to participate in an ISS assembly mission and to board the Space Station. Currently, she works as a CAPCOM (Spacecraft Communicator) at Mission Control Center in Houston. The CAPCOM is responsible for all communications between ground controllers and the astronauts in flight.

I believe that *effort* pays. Normal, daily, *consistent* effort. I believe in the simple truth that no matter the constraints or hurdles, determination and perseverance, if accompanied with some dose of humility, will get me further along my chosen path. I believe that if I want something strongly enough and that I am prepared to work for it, almost *anything* is possible.

Naturally I didn't come up with this belief on my own. I got help early on in life. When I was a kid, whenever I'd come home with a report card or with the news of some kind of achievement, my Mom, Jacqueline, would listen attentively. She'd say good work, well done, or something like that, but then she would *invariably* add, "but remember ma petite fille, there is always room for improvement." No matter how good the report was or how happy I felt about myself, *every single time*, without fail, my Mom would say, "sure, but there is still room for improvement."

Back then, I must confess that it annoyed me a little. After all, there *had* to be times when I had done my absolute very best, right? There had to be times when I *couldn't* possibly have done better.

But as I grew older, my Mom's saying kept resounding in my head and eventually, I came up with an interpretation that became part of my everyday motivation. I came to realize that there is no such thing as a free lunch and that great things can only be achieved if I put my heart to it. *Of course*, nobody is perfect and there is always room for improvement, but I might as well be glad that I am *aware* of it, choose what is right for me, strive for excellence, and enjoy every moment along the way. Effort, after all, does not necessarily have to be painful.

This philosophy may not work for everyone. Some seem to do minimum effort and still lead a fine life, while others struggle every day with little reprieve and few rewards. And someone clever once pointed out that the road to success is dotted with many *tempting* parking places.

True enough. But that is not a reason to give up and stand still.

Sure, it is easier to let things happen than to force them, easier to wait for opportunities rather than to create them. It is more convenient to blame circumstances than to try to change them, and there is *no doubt* that it is simpler to settle for the lowest common denominator or for the class average. In some cases, it is probably OK too.

But in *my book*, to make it *anywhere*, to reach that *personal dream*, climb that *coveted mountain*, or ride that *mighty rocket to space*, I know of only one basic recipe.

With a bit of effort, even the world can be at your feet....

For *This I Believe*, I am Julie Payette at the NASA-Johnson Space Center in Houston, Texas.

Reflecting

Communicating Effectively: How does the speaker's decision to emphasize certain words help you to determine the main message?

Metacognition: How does listening carefully to oral presentations make you a better speaker?

Critical Literacy: How do you think various audiences would respond to this radio essay differently? For example, an audience of astronauts versus an audience of students?

How to

Create DVD Covers

DVD covers are media texts, just like the movie within those covers. **All** media texts have a **clear purpose** and an **intended audience**. This information is important, not only when analyzing or consuming media, but when you are creating it. Follow these steps to create an effective DVD cover for an existing movie or a movie you would like to see produced.

1. Clearly define your purpose and audience. When creating a DVD cover, you're probably trying to get people interested in your movie. To accomplish this, you need to be clear on who your DVD is intended for. Who is most likely to find the movie appealing?

2. Create a title and other information (subtitles, names, reviews, ratings) targeted at your specific audience. Check out the type of information that appears on other DVD covers.

3. Choose images that will appeal to your audience and convey the message you want to send about your movie.

4. Experiment with the use of colour and different fonts and font sizes. This sort of element can convey mood, so your choices need to reflect your content. For example, if your movie is called *The Twilight Knights*, you might use images and background colours with a lot of blacks and reds. As well, you might choose between several different fonts that give the right feel for the setting (Middle Ages).

5. Remember that most DVD covers are a standard size. A DVD is usually 13.5 cm wide by 19 cm high. Create a template (a blank box) using these measurements. All your text and images must fit within these margins. Try to arrange text within these margins as effectively as possible.

6. Show a first draft of your cover to a few other people to get their opinion. Use their feedback to help you develop your final draft.

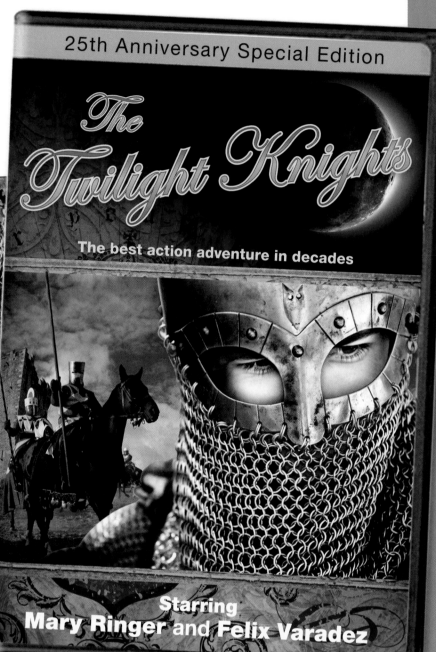

25th Anniversary Special Edition

The Twilight Knights

The best action adventure in decades

Starring
Mary Ringer and **Felix Varadez**

Transfer Your Learning

Across the Strands

Writing: Which of these steps do you follow when you're writing a story?

Across the Curriculum

Science: Imagine you were asked to create a DVD cover for a documentary called *Our Changing Seas*. What image would you choose?

Talk About It

What information do you look for when you examine a DVD cover?

Developing Zappit

Explanation by Erynn Ferguson

Creating DVD Covers →

Clearly define your purpose and audience. What is Erynn's purpose? Who is her audience?

I created a short 5-minute long, animated movie called *Zappit* for a school project. It was about my pet lizard and the way its tongue darts out so quickly to eat we've called it Zappit. When I created the DVD cover I wanted to get my classmates interested in watching my movie and tell them a bit about it, too. I knew the cover had to make a good first impression.

Zappit

Creating DVD Covers →

Create a title and other information targeted at your specific audience. Experiment with the use of colour and with different sizes and styles of type. What decisions has Erynn made about the text on her cover?

I knew the title *Zappit* was going to be quite large and green on my cover, just like my lizard. I checked out other DVD covers and the information they included. That's how I came up with the line "The lizard that ate everything" for the bottom of the cover.

Zappit
The lizard that ate everything

I had lots of great images to choose from for the cover. Finally, I decided that a simple drawing of Zappit's tongue would work best.

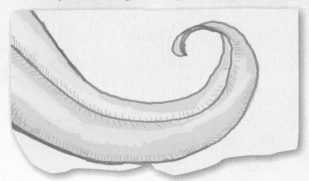

I put everything I had together and played around with my ideas a bit. I was pretty pleased with the first draft of my cover.

← **Creating DVD Covers**

Choose images that will appeal to your audience and convey the message you want to send about your movie. What message does Erynn convey with her choice of image? What other image might have been as effective?

← **Creating DVD Covers**

Try to arrange text and images as effectively as possible. Show a first draft of your cover to a few other people to get their opinion. What's your opinion on the effectiveness of this cover?

Reflecting

Creating Media Texts: What piece of advice for creating DVD covers do you consider most useful?

Metacognition: How do you know when you're ready to publish something or if it still needs more work? What process do you follow to help you decide?

Connecting to Other Media: What have you learned from examining other DVD covers that would help you create your own DVD cover?

Talk About It

In your opinion, what makes a DVD cover effective?

Zappit

DVD Cover by Erynn Ferguson

Here's the final draft of my DVD cover. I got some good advice to help me with the front cover. Then I decided I wanted to do a back cover with more information.

This 5-minute animated short tells the story of a lizard that just won't stop eating. Will he eat *anything*? Will he ever *stop* eating? Are *any* snacks safe from Zappit?

Script by Erynn Ferguson

Drawings by Erynn Ferguson

Narration by Erynn Ferguson

Produced by Erynn Ferguson

Sound Effects by Zappit

Music by Eric Ferguson

Rated PG

Reflecting

Creating DVD Covers: How effective is Erynn's cover for its purpose and audience?

Metacognition: What have you learned from examining the last two selections that can help you create your own DVD cover?

Problem/Solution

A problem/solution text pattern explains a problem and then suggests how it can be solved. For example, in a personal anecdote someone might explain how he or she made a terrible first impression the first day of class (the problem), and then how he or she worked to turn that impression around in the following days (the solution).

Here's an outline for the example given above.

Problem	→	**Reason**	→	**Solution**
Made a bad impression		Fell over my own feet		Showed everyone how good I was at sports

The problem/solution text pattern is used in informational texts such as political speeches and news articles. The pattern is usually structured in the following way:

1. The problem is stated in a topic sentence (sometimes there may be more than one problem).

2. A bit of detail about the problem is given.

3. One or more solutions are suggested.

4. A clincher sentence sums up the proposed solutions (optional).

Key words connected with this pattern are

• problem, solution

• solved, resolved

• the evidence shows, the issues are

• propose, conclude, steps can be taken

Transfer Your Learning

Across the Strands

Media Literacy: You may have noticed reporters sometimes use a problem/solution text pattern. What was the last news item you heard reported this way? What was the problem? What was the solution?

Across the Curriculum

Geography: Problem/solution text pattern is used often in geography. When reading about a serious problem such as overpopulation or disease control, how does understanding the problem/solution text pattern help you make sense of the text?

PEACE IT TOGETHER

Israelis and Palestinians Make Films on Canadian Soil

Newspaper article by Manusha Janakiram

Problem/Solution Text Pattern →

Problem/solution text pattern begins with a topic sentence that states the problem. What is the problem explored in this newspaper article?

Talk about the conflict in the Middle East rarely includes the word *collaboration*. However, for 29 youth gathered on Galiano Island in British Columbia, collaboration has been their mantra for the past two weeks.

"Each teenager from the other side thinks differently about the history and the government," said Ofir Vaknin, a Jewish resident of Dimona, Israel, in a phone interview. "It gave us a chance to listen to the other side and to know what they think about us."

"It's about listening to new perspectives," said Alaa Abu Dawoud, a Palestinian from Majd El Kurum in Israel. The two 17-year-olds joined other youth from Israel, Palestine, and Canada in creative conversations and filmmaking projects that aim to tell their stories—those of everyday people—about the conflict.

Entitled Peace It Together, the 18-day summer project is a joint effort between Creative Peace Network (CPN), a Vancouver-based multicultural charity, and the Gulf Islands Film and Television School of Galiano Island (GIFTS).

Problem/Solution Text Pattern →

Once the problem is identified, more information is usually provided to explain the problem more fully. What information here makes the problem clearer for the reader?

Peace It Together seeks to promote peace in the war-torn area "by building a culture of mutual respect and understanding between Palestinians, Israelis, Jews, Muslims, and Arabs."

Adri Hamael (left) and Reena Lazar

Dawoud added, "It's independent media—not affected by governments; it's our objective to show both sides of the story and let people make up their [own] minds."

According to CPN executive director Adri Hamael, "Through dialogue and filmmaking, the youth and their audiences [had] the chance to struggle with and make sense of the conflict that impacts so many lives."

Problem/Solution Text Pattern →

One or more solutions are provided to the problem. What solutions are offered by the Peace It Together camp?

Since it began in 2004, CPN has focused on building bridges toward peace in the Middle East. Inspired by similar programs around the world, the Peace It Together camp uses the arts, teamwork, and dialogue for creative initiatives.

This year CPN chose filmmaking "because it's a great way to teach the youth about constructive communication and teamwork and to help them realize how much power they have to change their world," said CPN's other executive director, Reena Lazar.

Dawoud said, "You will think for the future and try to have a better one."

Kenna Fair, the school's director, said, "We feel a responsibility as artists and communicators to put our resources to work so we can better our societies."

One such artist is award-winning documentary filmmaker Velcrow Ripper. As co-founder of GIFTS, Ripper believes that society needs stories of hope, possibility, and reconciliation in light of the violence and bloodshed plaguing the Middle East.

"Peace It Together is one such flower rising from the wreckage," Ripper said.

Misunderstanding is one of several challenges the teens faced throughout the intensive camp. As 18-year-old Ira Johnson of West Vancouver observed, "It's been very difficult. We're dealing with a lot of heavy issues."

But through dialogue, listening exercises, leadership training, and wilderness experiences, the teenagers found they were better able to cope with the many challenges they faced.

Regardless of whether or not the films from Peace It Together influence the decisions of government or military officials, Lazar said, "The participants [had] the unique opportunity to work through their fear and anger in a safe environment and with the very people to whom their feelings are directed."

The seven films were showcased at a gala event hosted in Vancouver a few days after the camp ended.

After the grand finale, participants returned home, hopefully to continue the collaborations they started on Galiano. As Vaknin said, "When I get back, I can help move things along … I think we all can."

Velcrow Ripper adds, "Canadians make fun of the fact that we are considered 'polite' and 'nice,'" he says. "But peace is a gift that we have to offer the world."

Participants in the program complete a film.

Problem/Solution Text Pattern

Key words, such as *solved* or *resolved*, can indicate problem/solution text pattern. What key words does this article use?

Problem/Solution Text Pattern

This text pattern sometimes ends with a concluding sentence that sums up the solution. What do you think is the most powerful concluding sentence for this article?

Reflecting

Analyzing Text Patterns: In your opinion, how clearly does this article state the problem and the solution? Support your answer.

Metacognition: How does thinking of the text pattern help you understand the text?

Talk About It

You have a lot more power than you may realize to influence the advertising aimed at you.

Made You Look

Article by Shari Graydon

Say your favourite group or singer is coming to town, and you're saving up to buy a ticket.

When you're thinking about what it will be like to attend the concert, do you get more excited about hearing the band and watching the light show or buying a T-shirt? A lot of advertisers assume you want the T-shirt. A concert promoter named John Roberts once said, "If a kid went to a concert and there wasn't any merchandise to buy, he'd probably go out of his mind." Talk about stereotyping!

Sometimes the assumptions that advertisers make about what's important to kids are wrong. Have you ever seen an ad that showed kids your age playing with some toy that you're way beyond and wondered, "What were they thinking?"

Unclear on the Concept

What's the best way to get advertisers who underestimate you to smarten up? Get in touch and let them know what you really like or don't like.

Young people are important to advertisers—they're always on the lookout for new ways to reach you and sell you stuff. The good news about this is that it means they care what you think. If you take the time to give them feedback, chances are they'll listen.

You have power. Let's call the power you have the "Three C's": Consumer Power, Companion Power, and Complaint Power. And you're in charge of how and when they get used.

Consumer Power

Every time you pull a quarter or a dollar or ten dollars out of your pocket, you're using your "consumer power." You're deciding how and where and on what you're going to spend your money.

But what then? What if you buy a game that falls apart after two weeks even though you used it exactly like the kid in the TV commercial did? Do you shove it to the back of your closet and then forget about it? Do you take it back to the store and request a refund? Or do you make a mental note of the name of the company that made it, and remind yourself to avoid wasting your money on their games in the future?

This last option is called a "boycott"—it refers to the decision people make to refuse to do business with a particular organization. In the past, people have boycotted TV stations for broadcasting too much violence; they've boycotted food and clothing companies for taking advantage of poor people in less fortunate countries; and they've boycotted perfume and beer advertisers for producing commercials and magazine ads that portrayed women as if they were objects to be bought and sold, instead of human beings.

Does it make much of a difference to a company if you stop buying their products or watching their shows? Maybe not, if you're the only one. But it's still worthwhile. Your choice to boycott gives you a way to say, "I think this company is irresponsible and dishonest. I don't support what they're doing or saying, and I'm going to do something—however small— to protest."

On the other hand, if you want your protest to make an even bigger difference—to change the way a company makes its toys or advertises its products—Companion Power and Complaint Power are good ways to increase your impact.

Companion Power

Say you're at a hockey or basketball game, and you stand up with your arms raised over your head. The only people likely to notice are the folks sitting next to you, or behind you. But if a whole bunch of people stand up all together or in a "wave," everybody notices!

The same principle applies when it comes to consumer protest. If you see an ad on TV that makes Ramma Gamma X Star look like the greatest game ever, but you know from experience that it's actually really boring and nothing like the ad suggests, you're likely to tell all your friends. Then if your friends tell their brothers and sisters, who tell their own friends, who then tell even more people … well, you get the picture—it's like "the wave" at the sports event—it's pretty hard to ignore! A "wave" of consumer power—in which a lot of "companions" stop buying products—is more likely to get noticed.

Complaint Power

If you *really* want the company to change what it's doing—in the ad, at its manufacturing plant, or in another country—the best thing to do is talk to the company directly. A phone call is more powerful than simply telling your friends, and an e-mail is even better, but companies take letters that come through the mail most seriously of all. A letter seems more real somehow; it's harder for people to throw it away than it is for them to delete an e-mail or phone message. And a letter takes more time to write than an e-mail or phone call, so companies know the writer is serious. If more than one person writes to a company expressing concern about the same thing—combining Companion Power and Complaint Power—that's even better!

Zapped

Here's just one example of Complaint Power in action: a TV ad for long-distance phone service hoped to encourage former residents of rural areas who still had relatives living there to "phone home." The commercial showed a wheat field buzzing with mosquitoes. The voice-over said: "You may not want to travel there, but you can at least phone. Save 25 percent on long-distance calls." But some people who saw the ad felt insulted by it. They thought the commercial was suggesting that these areas were unappealing places to live or visit. As a result of four complaints, the phone company cancelled the commercial.

Can You Imagine How Powerful Those People Felt?

Often people are surprised to learn that a company will cancel an ad in response to just a few complaints from a handful of people. However, advertisers recognize that for every person who picks up the phone or writes a letter to complain, there are probably hundreds more who are also offended. Smart advertisers often decide to pull the ad that caused concern right away rather than risk angering other potential customers.

Getting Companies to Listen Up

Some complainers are more effective than others. You may have noticed this in life generally: Two people can have exactly the same problem with the way something is being done. They can both complain about the problem, but sometimes one person gets the brush-off while the other one gets an apology or a refund.

It often comes down to that old expression, "You can catch more flies with honey than vinegar." As your parents and teachers have probably told you, being polite pays off. Using the sweet approach (honey) is usually more effective than using the sour approach (vinegar).

Here's how it works. Say you hear an ad for a new soft drink on the radio. In trying to be humorous, the ad makes fun of a person with a lisp. You think the ad is mean-spirited and unfair—that it encourages kids to pick on someone who's different. Instead of just concentrating on your own anger, you have to approach the advertiser in a way that ensures the company will take you seriously. In the letter that you write to the radio station and to the soft drink company, you'll want to point out the following:

1. You listen to and like the radio station. This tells the station that you are part of their regular audience, and reminds them that they rely on your attention in order to attract advertisers.

2. You drink pop. This tells the advertiser that you are exactly the kind of person they're trying to persuade to try the new soda.

3. You are offended by the commercial. Here you'll want to explain what you don't like about the ad in a calm and clear manner. The more polite and reasonable you sound, the more likely they are to pay attention to your feedback.

4. You won't buy the soda as long as they air this ad. You're exercising your "Consumer Power," in a way that tells them the ad is backfiring!

5. You'll consider boycotting the radio station if the ad continues, which means you won't hear any of their other customers' ads, either!

6. You're planning to encourage friends and family to follow your lead. This shows that you can gather together some "Companion Power," too.

7. You'd like a written response from both the radio station and the advertiser demonstrating that they understand your concerns, and telling you how they're going to act. This makes it more difficult for them to ignore your letter. And if they have to go to the trouble of writing a response, they'll have to either figure out a way to defend their ad, or make a commitment to pulling it off the air.

Finally, when you sign the letter, you might also consider telling the station and company how old you are. Because not very many kids write to companies, this will make it easier for your letter to get noticed.

It's always a good idea to send your letter to both the advertiser and to its media "host"—the TV or radio station, magazine or newspaper, billboard company, bus line, blog, or website—that allowed the ad to be seen or heard in the first place. And if you can afford the extra stamps, you might also send copies of your letter to the organization in your country in charge of advertising rules.

Don't Try This at Home!

Patent medicines that claimed they could cure everything from headaches to stomach ulcers were banned decades ago. And yet some advertisers still make promises that sound pretty unbelievable. If you see an ad that makes a claim you think sounds fishy, you can write to the company asking for proof. Be clear that you're looking for evidence that's been gathered in a scientific way. And make sure you tell them you don't simply want more advertising. Sometimes people making such requests have received a whole whack of promotional brochures—in other words, more claims!—instead of actual proof.

Reflecting

Analyzing Text Pattern: How does the organization of this article help you understand its information? How did the headings help?

Metacognition: How helpful is this article in getting you to think more critically about advertising?

Connecting to Other Media: When you make a decision to buy something, how much are you influenced by the advertising for that product?

Talk About It
Are pro sports teams fair to everyone?

A League of Her Own

Interview by James Prime

Until 1943, baseball's policy was "No girls allowed!" Women were banned from professional baseball in 1931 after a 17-year-old pitcher named Jackie Mitchell struck out Lou Gehrig and Babe Ruth in an exhibition game. After that, embarrassed by the incident, the baseball commissioner claimed that baseball was "too strenuous" for women.

Then along came World War II. With so many men off fighting, women took over many traditionally male jobs, and proved they could excel given the chance. When professional male baseball players were recruited for the war too, the owner of the Chicago Cubs, P.K. Wrigley, saw an opportunity: distract people from the war by starting an all-women baseball league. In 1943, the All-American Girls Professional Baseball League was formed. The movie *A League of Their Own* was based on their story.

This is the story of one of its stars: Annabelle Lee.

Annabelle Lee pitched in the AAGPBL for seven seasons with an impressive lifetime ERA (earned run average) of .225. She is now 85 years old and has lost none of her enthusiasm for baseball, or for life.

JIM: How did you get your start in professional baseball?

ANNABELLE: In 1944, I was playing fast-pitch softball in Hollywood, California, and the league sent a scout to look at various ballplayers. They chose about 10 of us to go and try out. They offered me $85 a week to do something that I loved. So I accepted. We had the tryouts in Peru, Illinois, and I was one of the lucky ones to make it.

JIM: How did the league get started?

ANNABELLE: It was in the midst of World War II and people needed an escape from all the bad news, the food rationing, and the worry about loved ones fighting overseas. That was why Chicago Cubs owner P.K. Wrigley started the league in '43. The military were taking so many boys from the big leagues and making them join the service—stars like Ted Williams and Joe DiMaggio, and dozens of others. He wanted something for the people to enjoy while this was going on. They set up franchises in smaller cities instead of the big centres like New York and Boston.

JIM: Was it an immediate success?

ANNABELLE: In 1943 there were four teams. In 1945 there were six. The attendance grew every year. The league drew about 175 000 fans the first year, and by 1948 it was almost a million. The first three years they pitched fast-pitch underhand but they played baseball rules—smaller ball and longer bases and pitching distance.

JIM: How high was the calibre of play in your league?

ANNABELLE: Very high! It was much higher than it is now for women's hardball.

JIM: Were the league rules strict?

ANNABELLE: We had so many rules. Oh, boy, did we ever! They were very strict. We had our chaperones. They were like our mentors, and they watched to see that we obeyed the rules. There were time restrictions. We had to be in our rooms on time. We had to be in the hotel by two hours after games. We couldn't wear slacks on the street. The manager would sit in the lobby of the hotel to make sure we were all in. Of course, there were a few who didn't follow all the rules. They'd stay out later and then find a way to sneak in.

JIM: Were you one of them?

ANNABELLE: No. The thing is, we were so involved with baseball and we loved it so much. After the games we'd have our meetings at the park, but then we girls would meet in one room and discuss the games ourselves—what we did wrong and what we should have done. We took it very seriously. We were dedicated.

JIM: Did you consider yourself a pioneer?

ANNABELLE: Not at the time. We didn't feel that way really. We were only doing what we loved. We didn't know anything about that until the movie (*A League of Their Own*) came out. Then people started to say, "Oh, you're the pioneers who opened the door for women. If it wasn't for you, the girls wouldn't be as far along in sports as they are right now." We were happy about that, but when you are part of history you sometimes don't see it as history. I didn't feel like anything was special about it at that time. Even today I have trouble thinking about it in those terms because it was something we loved to do.

I played baseball, hardball, and softball for 20 years from 1937 to 1957. It was just something you did, not something you thought you were doing to help somebody out—except your team.

JIM: You were role models for many girls of the time.

ANNABELLE: At card shows, we've had a lot of women come up to thank us. It's funny, but also a lot of young boys would thank us as well. They saw it as an issue of fairness. They appreciated what we did and didn't know how we did it. They were glad that a change had been made. They were fascinated to meet the women who had gone through that.

JIM: What was life on the road like for a team of female ballplayers? What sort of problems did you face?

ANNABELLE: The first team I played on, in Minneapolis, lost their franchise and we had to play all our games on the road. We were in Milwaukee and we got word there that we weren't going back to Minnesota. We only had two days' worth of clothes in our suitcases and we couldn't go back to get them until after the season.

ANNABELLE "LEFTY" LEE

All we did was travel on buses to the ballparks: Racine, Wisconsin, Fort Wayne, Indiana. We had to do our own washing. At that time there were no washers or dryers so we had to do our washing in the bathtubs and let the laundry dry in the windows. Sometimes the stockings were hung out the bus windows. It must have been quite a sight for other motorists.

If we wanted to wear jeans or slacks we had to roll them up and wear skirts over the top or wear a long coat because we weren't allowed out in public like that.

We thought then that it was going too far and I still do today. But that was the rule and we had to abide by them if we wanted to play baseball. The bottom line was we were supposed to be the "All-American girls next door"—wholesome and all that.

JIM: So it was a pretty tough life?

ANNABELLE: It was pretty hard with the long hours on the road and then playing and everything. We had to practise in the mornings too—and then go to the ballpark in the afternoon.

Peoria to Grand Rapids was an eight-hour bus trip. If you didn't sleep on the bus you were in trouble because you couldn't go to your room. You hung around the lobby and waited. No showers or anything. We often couldn't shower after a game because we had to get right on the bus and leave for the next town and the next game. So we waited for the next town. But we loved every minute of it. All in all it was worth it. It made my life richer. I wish you could see my room with the memorabilia everywhere. I'm surrounded by wonderful memories.

JIM: What accomplishment are you most proud of?

ANNABELLE: In 1944 I pitched the first perfect game in league history. That was in Kenosha, Kansas. The only thing I remember about the game is that nobody said a word. My teammates came back to the bench after every inning and didn't say a word to me. I didn't know anything special had happened until after the game. They were very superstitious and didn't want to jinx me.

I was traded to Fort Wayne the following year and that's when I pitched a no-hitter against Grand Rapids. The first perfect game was underhand, this one was overhand.

One of the best things was going to Cuba. We picked up five Cuban players. There was a U.S. all-star team and a Cuban team and we played each other. We barnstormed (in small planes) from California to Mexico City to Nicaragua to Costa Rica to Panama to Aruba, and then Venezuela, Puerto Rico, and Cuba. Then we flew back home—after three months.

JIM: Your uniform was on display in the Hall of Fame. That's quite an honour.

ANNABELLE: Yes, it was exhibited in Cooperstown, New York, for five years or more. My shoes and hat are still in Cooperstown, but the uniform is now on a bus that tours the U.S. and stops to exhibit in different cities. They show people what it was like for women to play in those days. It's en route somewhere all the time.

JIM: What difference has baseball made in your life?

ANNABELLE: It made me recognize other people from other countries, different nationalities and cultures, different ways of life, and to accept everyone for what they are and try to do good. It taught me to accept people the way they are, and not the way I want them to be.

Bill Lee is a former professional baseball player who pitched for the Montréal Expos and the Boston Red Sox. Annabelle Lee is his aunt.

Bill: Aunt Annabelle was the best athlete in our family and the best baseball player. My father and my aunt taught me how to pitch.

JIM: Do you consider your aunt to be a pioneer?

Bill: Yes. She and her teammates opened the door for a lot of other women. It takes courage to be the first at anything. She was a great fan favourite and drew people to the ballpark. In fact, whenever a new franchise was added to the league, they would bring her in to help drum up more interest.

JIM: Do you think she faced discrimination?

Bill: Sure she did. They lost their ballpark the first year because some minor league owner refused to share his field. They were forced to play all of their games on the road that season because they had no home ballpark. The bus became their home. They used to hang their stockings out the windows to dry.

JIM: Your aunt sounds pretty stubborn. How do you think she handled all these rules?

Bill: Well, I know she was the first to cut her dress down and make it into a mini-skirt. She couldn't throw so well with the longer dress so she altered it to free up her delivery.

JIM: So she and her fellow ballplayers made an impact on society?

Bill: Definitely. At the time she played, women could really only dream of being teachers and nurses. They are both wonderful professions but the door was closed on so many other careers. The women of this league showed that women can survive and excel in what were traditionally male roles.

The Canadian Connection

It may have been called the All-American Girls Professional Baseball League, but it had a large Canadian crowd. Approximately 10% of the players were from Canada. They were all inducted into the Canadian Baseball Hall of Fame in 1998. Here are just a few of the stars.

- Mary "Bonnie" Baker was quite a catch for the AAGPBL. The Saskatchewan native's eight brothers and sisters were all catchers. With her husband overseas fighting, she joined the league in 1943 and vowed to return home when her husband did. She was a two-time all-star catcher for the South Bend Blue Sox. She was chosen to pose for posters advertising the league and became the face of the women's game.

- Vancouver's Helen Callaghan played in the outfield for the Fort Wayne Daisies and won the batting title in the AAGPBL in 1945, batting .299. She was known as the Ted Williams of women's baseball. She is often credited as the inspiration for the movie *A League of Their Own.*

- Olive Bend Little of Manitoba established an unbeaten strikeout record while throwing four no-hitters. Her career (1943–1945) was short but spectacular.

- Gladys Terry Davis was a shortstop who hailed from Toronto—she captured the first batting championship in the AAGPBL, batting .332 for the Rockford Peaches in 1943.

Reflecting

Metacognition: What strategies do you use to achieve a goal that at first seems unattainable?

Critical Thinking: When reading a story about a real person, what is the advantage to using photos of that individual? What other artifacts would help you appreciate his or her life?

Connecting to Other Media: As with many historical events, this story was made into a Hollywood movie. Is it important that these movies be 100% accurate? Is it even possible?

NEL

A League of Her Own   113

The Arts

The reading strategy you learned in this unit can help you to better understand text in other subject areas. As you read, ask yourself questions to evaluate these images and the text.

An Artist Comes to Canada

Art Exhibit by Gu Xiong

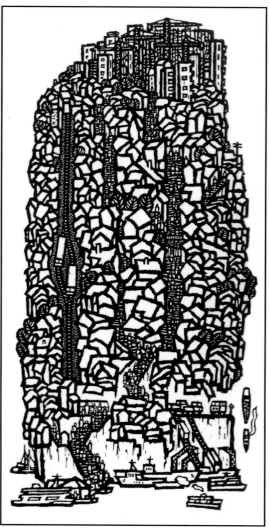

Gu Xiong, *Chongqing*, 1984, woodblock print

Artist Gu Xiong tells the story of growing up in China during the 1950s and '60s knowing Canada only from the paintings of the Group of Seven. He says of these paintings, "This was my first impression of Canada. I dreamed to visit those white mountains."

Years later, Gu Xiong immigrated to Canada. Of that experience, he says, "In 1989, I came to Canada after the Tiananmen Square Massacre*. My dreams for China were crushed by tanks. In Canada, my dreams were also crushed by reality. But my new life was born after my old life was gone. It was like sinking to the bottom of the ocean and resurfacing. I had no choice but to face my situation and strive to become a better person through my struggling between cultures."

*Tiananmen Square Massacre: a protest by democracy supporters in Beijing in 1989, in which hundreds of protesters were killed by Chinese soldiers.

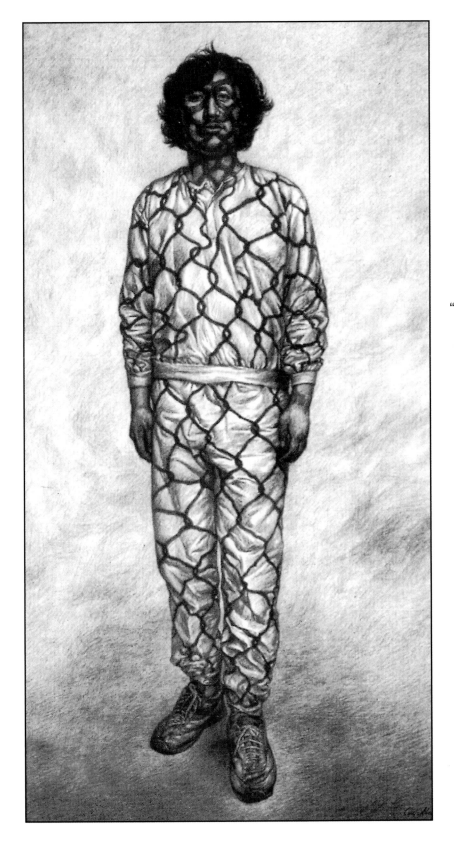

Gu Xiong, *Enclosure*,
1995, charcoal on canvas

"People make enclosures for
themselves. We can't see most
of them; they are so common,
they become invisible. Many
of these enclosures are inside
of us. I hope that one day we
can discard them, to better
comprehend ourselves, and
to awaken the link between
humanity and nature, between
one person and another."

— Gu Xiong

Home
Poem by Gu Xiong

My family
Under the clouds
Moves from one land to another
Struggling between cultures
Not knowing to which we belong

Even though the flowers are falling
The fruit will appear later
When the maple leaves rest on the ground
My family finally settles down

We are like seeds in the depths of this land
Absorbing fresh water and light
Straining to put down roots
But blossoming will soon follow
And then at last bearing fruit

A flower
A leaf
A cloud
A deep breath
Bringing with it
A new life.

Gu Xiong, *Behold the Silence*,
1995, charcoal on canvas

Reflecting on the Text

Evaluating: What message does the artist send with his poem and artwork? Do you agree with this artist's message?

Metacognition: How did the text help you understand and evaluate the artwork?